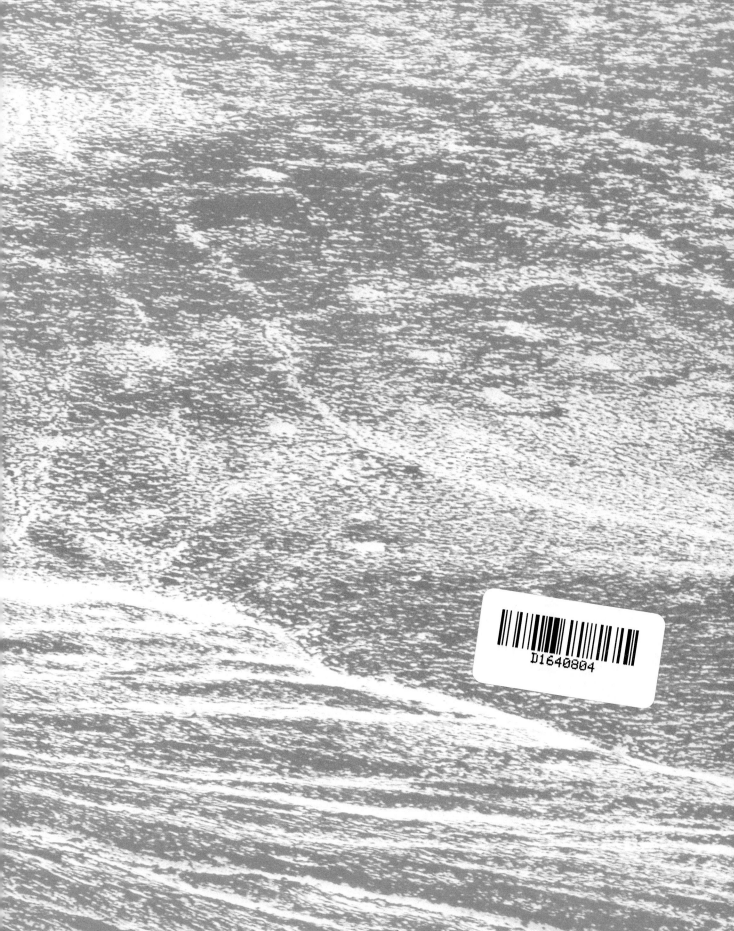

TONGARIRO
A SACRED GIFT

Photographs and Text: Craig Potton
Overwriting, European history and editing: Andy Dennis
Maori History: Veronica Black
Ecology: Kevin Hackwell

TONGARIRO
A SACRED GIFT

A Centennial Celebration of Tongariro National Park
WRITTEN AND PHOTOGRAPHED BY
CRAIG POTTON

Published jointly by Lansdowne Press and Craig Potton

Dedicated to Bruce and Margaret, Paul and Diane,
who made me feel at home at Tongariro, and Beverly,
who accompanied me in all kinds of weather.

Project Co-ordinator: Barbara Nielsen
Park Logistics: Bruce Jefferies and Paul Dale
Overwriting: Andy Dennis
Text Editor: Jeanette Cook
Typing: Beverly Baseman
Design: Piers Hayman
Typeset by ATS, Auckland
Printed in Hong Kong by Everbest Printing Co. Ltd
Published by Lansdowne Press
a division of Weldon Pty Ltd
59 View Road, Glenfield
Auckland, New Zealand
and
Craig Potton,
Box 555, Nelson, New Zealand
© Craig Potton and Lansdowne Press
First published 1987
ISBN 0-86866-110-4

All rights reserved. No part of this publication may be reproduced, stored in a retrieval system, or transmitted in any form, or by any means, electronic, mechanical, photocopying, recording, or otherwise, without the prior written permission of the publisher.

CONTENTS

FOREWORD Sir Hepi Te Heuheu	8
INTRODUCTION Bruce Jefferies	9
FIRE Forces of volcanism	18
ICE, WATER AND WIND Forces of erosion	62
LIFE The ecology of the park	76
PEOPLE Maori and European history	122
SACREDNESS AND PROTECTION Philosophies of land use	150
MAP Tongariro National Park	190
ACKNOWLEDGEMENTS	191
FURTHER READING	192
GLOSSARY Maori concepts and place names	192

FOREWORD

Sir Hepi Te Heuheu stands beside his Tuwharetoa ancestral pole at the Waihi Marae, Taupo.

Welcome to Tongariro. One hundred years ago my great-grandfather, Horonuku Te Heuheu Tukino IV gifted the sacred summits of Tongariro on behalf of the Tuwharetoa to the Government to protect their tapu. In so doing he and his people established a three way bond between land, Maori and Pakeha. The gift says these sacred mountains are to be owned by no-one and yet are for everyone. My Tuwharetoa people wish the gift to be remembered for all time. The mountains of the south wind have spoken to us for centuries. Now we wish them to speak to all who come in peace and in respect of their tapu. This land of Tongariro National Park is our mutual heritage. It is a gift given many times over. As each of us receives it we could in spirit join Ngatoroirangi of the Arawa canoe, Ariki ancestor of Tuwharetoa, in his invocation when he first landed in this country.

   Ka u ki matanuku,
   Ka u ki Matarangi;
   Ka u ki tenei whenua,
   Hei whenua,
   Mau e kai te manawa o tauhou!
I arrive where unknown earth is under my feet,
I arrive where a new sky is above me;
I arrive at this land, a resting place for me;
O Spirit of the Earth! The stranger
humbly offers his heart as food for You!

Sir Hepi Te Heuheu

INTRODUCTION

The crater of Mt Ngauruhoe.

Tongariro and Ruapehu are mountains sacred to the Maori who have lived at their feet for almost a thousand years. In 1887 Te Heuheu Tukino IV, the paramount chief of the Tuwharetoa, gifted on behalf of his tribe the summits of Tongariro and part of Ruapehu to the people of New Zealand, so that their tapu might be protected for all time.

This gift was made towards the end of a century which had witnessed massive destruction of natural landscapes and indigenous cultures in many parts of the world. Yet in that time of expanding frontiers and rampant industrialism other social ideals were beginning to gain acceptance. A combination of democracy and Romantic culture gave the vision and means to preserve large areas of wilderness as the common heritage of all. The idea of a park belonging to the whole nation became a reality in 1872, at Yellowstone in the United States. Canada and Australia soon followed with parks of their own, and the basis for the world's fourth national park was laid by Te Heuheu Tukino's gift of Tongariro and Ruapehu in 1887. It was no accident that this innovation happened first in New World nations, which lacked cultural edifices to enshrine as national monuments but still had extensive tracts of unspoilt wilds.

For the mountains to remain sacred our generation must honour the intention behind the original Maori gift. Equally, we must heed the European philosophers, poets and conservationists who created and nourished the ideal of national parks. Beneath the speaking mountains our two cultures have come together and must continue to meet in a strong and creative relationship. Our task is to continue to cement the ancient bonds, and to guarantee future protection of the land, so that it may continue to speak of forces beyond us.

Bruce Jefferies
(Chief Ranger at Tongariro
National Park 1979-1986)

'From the first place of liquid darkness, within the second place of air and light, I set down the following record with its mixture of fact and truths and memories of truths and its direction always toward the Third Place, where the starting point is myth.'

To the Is-land, Janet Frame

Kati au, ka hoki
Ki toku whenua tupu,
Te wai-koropupu,
E ki a mai nei
I hu ra i Tongariro
E Ngatoro-i-rangi
Ma mahana ki tana kiri;
Na Rangi mai ano,
Nana i marena,
Ko Pihanga he wahine,
Ai hu, ai hau,
Ai marangai kiri.
Ki te muri e – i!
Kokiri e!

Cease, my sorrow, for now I go
To my childhood land,
My sacred land where fountains of
Enchantment rise from sacred fires,
From Tongariro's height where magic
Flames were kindled by Nga-toro-i-rangi
Fire that warmed the chieftain.
From heaven came those fires.
Pihanga Mountain was the wife,
Wedded with the ancient flame,
United in the smoky clouds
Breathed from the mountain's pit,
They embrace in the stormwind
Marangai.
So is my love to him I leave! . . .

This Maori Waiata is still sung locally by the Tuwharetoa.

OPENING THE BOOK

You open the book
& there unfolds a road   its skin is blue, it is summer
the heat   that dances in its hollows turns
into water.   You ride it in the vehicles of strangers:
homesteads & haybarns   dusty yellow sheeptrucks
convoy of soldiers in jungle greens returning

from an exercise   slipping
past their polarized windscreens;
you draw from them splinters   of lives made of words

though you never take your eyes off the mountains.
The mountains   reach out to embrace you
they fold their blue ankles

they give birth to rivers, they
can even crouch like tigers if that's the way you
want them: they are a story you tell

about yourself, a story you are journeying
into, which swallows you.   You leave
the road, then   you honour the logic of ridges

& gorges, of funnels, of slotted
stone chimneys   You startle a huge bird
nesting in the riverbed, climbing on slow

cream & ash coloured wings   & you follow
as it disappears
inland, you tunnel to the spine of the island &

bury yourself   alive, with your possessions, this
curved sky, this whisper of ice-cloud
this magic mountain slamming shut behind you.

John Newton

Minerals, algae and moss coat the rocks at Ketetahi Springs.

He waiata murimuri-aroha

Ka korikori ake i raro rā i te ata o Tongariro maunga
Ka tū au ka wawata, ko wai rā taku iwi
Ko wai rā taku ihi, taku wana, taku tū
Ka hoki ngā mahara, ki te pane o Pūtauaki
Kei tua ko te papa e arohatia nei e
He tohu i taku tūranga waewae, taku noho mauri-tau e

Ka rite ki te rimu teretere i te moana
Ka pari i te akau, te moana i Taupō
Tākiri ko te ata, mau mai ko ahau e tuohu noa ana e—
Ka aupaki kau ake, ki te ārai uhi mai
Kei tua ko koutou, e kui mā, e koro mā, e hika mā, e
tā mā e—
Ka huri ka titiro ki te ao whai muri e

He oha nā te whaea
E tipu te whakareanga nei, e tipu e
Nāku rā koe i rauhī, i here ki taku pito
Nāku anō koe i pēhi, rutu ake,
I maunu mai ai tō matihe
Tihe! i mauri ora
I ngāngā ai tō waha areare ki te ao mārama e-ai-a

Kōhine Whakarua Pōnika

A SONG OF YEARNING

Beneath the shadow of Tongariro mountain
I stir to a new surrounding
Thoughts fill with anxiety—where am I, who am I, and
all that I have left behind
The mind penetrates to the peak of Putauaki
Where it shadows from my view the land that I love
The place where I was born—my home sweet home

I'm classed as a seaweed now that drifts in the ocean to
be stranded by the waves, on the shores of Lake Taupo
Breaks the dawn, and I am caught, in meditation
A gesture of the hand, to an imaginary curtain that veils
the old folks, the dear ones, the loved ones, gone on
Then, I turn and cast my eyes on the young world,
moving in

A mother's last words
Grow, the young generation—grow
It was I who nurtured the seed, that was tied to my
navel
Again it was I who laboured for its rude awakening,
exhorting the sneeze of life, and the loud burst of the
lungs
To herald new entry into this world

Yellow flowering Ranunculus insignus, *mountain foxgloves and native tussocks at Soda Springs.*

Mt Ngauruhoe, during the 1975 eruption.

The 1969 Eruption on Mt Ruapehu.

FIRE

'IT LOOKED LIKE HELL'S KITCHEN'

On the 8th of May 1971 four men set out on a triangulation survey of Mt Ruapehu's Crater Lake. Using precise measurements between several fixed points around the rim of the lake scientists can determine if the land is rising or falling, and thus if an eruption is imminent. On this day Marshall Gebbie, a Mt Ruapehu local, went along with the scientists simply because he was fascinated by volcanoes.

About 8.00 am Otto Gram the helicopter pilot dropped John Latter, Chris Hewson, Peter Otway and myself (Marshall Gebbie) up at the Crater Lake. All day we went through the triangulation survey of the area. During the day we were visited by a television news team. While they were on the Dome with us at about midday, there was a 10 foot bubble (convolution) in the middle of the lake. After catching it on film they decided it would be strategic to shoot through, quickly.

We continued on and at the end of the survey Peter and I were on top of the Pyramid, a prominent tower of rock on the eastern edge of the Crater Lake. Practically overhanging the lake, there is about a 600 foot drop down into the lake from the top of the Pyramid. Between the drop and us we had a 2 foot ledge; the tripod and theodolite were set up immediately behind that. We had just completed the survey, it was 7 minutes to 4.00 pm, and I was puffing on my pipe. I remember watching the lake, chatting away with Peter who was fiddling with his gear, and I saw the surface of the lake dome:... it bulged and I thumped Peter and said something unprintable. He turned around and the thing opened up into a violent explosion almost 600 feet high. We dived for our cameras and managed to start taking pictures. It was a silent eruption; there was a vibration and as it came up we could hear rushing water. It then started to drop and great hunks of rock began falling out of it, but it was all contained and very entertaining; there was little fear involved.

The other two men at this stage were on the col between the Dome and the Pyramid, observing the eruption from a slightly safer position. Peter and I were almost directly downwind from the eruption. We started to jabber to each other in excitement after the eruption had subsided. Then there was an almighty, tremendous bang and the whole mountain shook. Spirals and great fingers of debris screamed skyward at a tremendous rate. It just kept going up and up and our whole field of vision was taken up with this 'thing' coming at us and going up into the air. We dropped the cameras. Peter grabbed the bench-mark (surveying peg) and threw himself down behind the little ridge, pulled his pack over his head and hung on. I grabbed my ice axe as I had no bench-mark to grab,

ABOVE: An explosion originating 1 km beneath Ruapehu's Crater Lake ejects water, mud, hot ash and partially molten rocks to a height of 800 m in May 1971.

slammed it into the ice, dropped flat onto my face, pulled my pack over my head and hung on.

The first thing I remember is the lake water hitting us. It just saturated us. So acidic was the water that it stung all the orifices of our bodies. We were completely engulfed. It washed my ice axe out and I started to go backwards down the steep slope very quickly. I scrambled to my knees and as I did I gave another almighty whack with my ice axe giving it every single thing I had. I pulled my pack up against myself and hung on.

Seconds later the ash hit us, blotting everything out. I had a little radio with me and was trying to call John Latter, but I couldn't even hear myself yelling into the radio. Every time I took a breath the ash would coat the inside of my mouth. There was ash, ash like you've never seen; you could hold your hand up in front of your face and it was completely black. I remember trying to put my mouth down inside my jersey to try and filter the ash, but it was still getting through and the poisonous hydrogen sulphide gas was starting to affect me. I called out to Peter—he was only a couple of feet away from me to my right— but there was nothing, no reply, he couldn't hear. Then I heard whistling noises, huge rocks coming down from a couple of thousand feet and landing all around us. One rock fell just about exactly where I had been lying. It would have taken off half my head if I hadn't slipped down the ice.

I thought it was curtains. I couldn't breathe for ash and I had started to go funny in the head with the gas. Then all of a sudden a freezing cold icy wind howled up behind us, which caused the cloud and ash to mushroom up and away from us. The eruption had blasted the surrounding air out, but when it stopped the displaced air rushed back up the slopes. It almost tasted like a fluid it was so clean and magnificent. I gulped this fresh air down and then clawed my way up and looked over the ledge and saw huge house-sized blocks whizzing around the lake like jet boats, bashing into each other; it looked like Hell's kitchen...

Glancing into Hell's kitchen, even at the risk of becoming an ingredient in the lethal soup, remains as seductive today as it did to the earliest of the colonial explorers. In 1839 John Bidwill was the first European to step up to the lip of the crater on Ngauruhoe and stare at 'the most terrific abyss that I ever looked into or imagined.' Since then many scientists and others have followed in his steps, journeying on pilgrimages tinged with fear and curiosity to seek answers from Tongariro National Park's hotlines to the earth's interior.

The interior of the earth is a nuclear reactor still running on heat left over from the planet's early solar evolution. South African mines, which have probed gold-bearing layers 4 km down into the earth, reveal a rise of 2 to 3°C for every 100 m increase in depth. Earthquake studies and laboratory experiments show a semi-molten layer below the earth's crust which is 1100-1200°C, and in the solid heart of the earth's inner core it is believed that temperatures reach 4300°C. Every day this deeply generated heat issues in steam from the craters and hot-spots in the park. Less frequently it explodes in massive eruptions.

The earth's inner cauldron drives processes which build mountains and cause the spreading of ocean floors. One scientist has found a useful analogy in the humble task of brewing jam. The element of the stove functions like the super-heated core of the earth from which molten rock (magma) rises in heat currents only to cool out on the surface and form a crust, like that found on slowly cooking jam. Parts of this crust are in turn carried to the edge of the cooking pot where they are pulled under and reheated. In a very general way this analogy is useful in understanding the outline of plate tectonics and continental drift, theories which account for both earthquakes and volcanoes in one coherent picture.

Floating on a hot interior mantle, the earth's surface consists of a solid crust of thick light rocks which make up the land masses and continental shelves, and a thinner layer of heavier rock which spreads across the deep ocean floors. The planet's surface consists of twelve large crustal plates (most containing both land and ocean crust) and several smaller ones. These plates float on a semi-molten layer which is continually extruding new material and

Eruption clouds laden with fine ash, tower above Ngauruhoe while heavier pyroclastic debris sweeps down the slopes during the 1974-75 eruptions.

The still active Red Crater on Mt Tongariro.

thus forcing the plates into collision courses. Typically, on one edge a major plate will be in the process of formation, in the course of which it gets pushed apart from its neighbouring plate along huge ocean ridge systems which extrude magma to form new crust in continuous volcanic upwelling. The enormous extent of new ocean crust formation is usually unseen and unheard except where it rises above sea level and sets about wrenching land apart, as happens in Iceland.

On other edges crustal plates crush into each other. New Zealand sits astride the collision course of two of the world's largest plates, the Indian-Australian and the Pacific plates. In the South Island these plates have collided at an angle, thrusting up sea sediments to form the still-rising Southern Alps, and skewing sideways to cause one of the planet's greatest faultlines - the Alpine Fault. Further to the north, some 60 km to 80 km off the East Coast of the North Island, the Pacific Plate dives below its Indian-Australian couterpart in a process called subduction. Although the point of subduction may be off-shore, many of the effects are on-shore, and nowhere is this more apparent than in the Taupo Volcanic Zone.

As the Pacific Plate dips beneath its Indian-Australian neighbour a giant conveyor belt of crustal basalts and waterlogged ocean sediments rides a downward-flowing convection current at the rate of about 5 cm a year. This mixture forms an explosive brew of steam, carbon dioxide gases and magma, and as the subducting crustal slab slides under at an angle of 30 to 70 degrees it carries this explosive brew down to regions of extremely high temperatures. While sinking, the slab gains heat primarily by conduction and friction, and at a critical depth starts to melt to produce molten diapirs (tear-drop shapes) of buoyant, gas-laden magma which rise towards the surface. These rising magma bubbles collect in large chambers near the surface and maintain internal heat over long periods. These are the furnaces that fire up to the surface through cracks and fissures to create the park's delightful and deadly displays of volcanism.

Lava rising to the surface as a vertical sheet formed this dyke in Red Crater. When the magma chamber lost pressure, the remaining lava in the dyke oozed back leaving this striking vertical cavern in the crater wall.

FORM AND CONTENT

'The more like a volcano your pile looks, the smaller the eruptions.'
George Walker, volcanologist.

When it comes to volcanoes and the landscapes they create, shape and type can be very misleading. Most people would probably think that Taranaki / Mt Egmont and Ngauruhoe are New Zealand's major volcanoes. They after all have the classic volcano form like Mts Fuji, St Helens or Vesuvius. And even if we are aware that Lake Taupo has some mysterious connection with the huge volumes of ash which cover the central North Island, it somehow seems more likely that Ruapehu, Ngauruhoe, Tarawera, Edgecumbe and White Island must have provided the biggest fireworks. Yet the present form of these volcanoes is very misleading.

When the earth opens up in and around Lake Taupo the eruptions exceed those at Ruapehu and Tongariro by an order of magnitude that is akin to comparing a nuclear bomb to a firecracker. A key to understanding this is the fact that the intensity of volcanic events is determined far more by the content of the material released than by the outward appearance of the volcano.

If magma from the earth's mantle manages to flow relatively unimpeded to the surface and remains uncontaminated by crustal material, it forms the 'basic' rock type called basalt. Basalt is low in silica and flows easily, more or less continuously, and therefore predictably. Most eruptions of basalt lava are commonly quiet affairs that bubble away undersea in mid-ocean trenches where crustal plates are being pushed apart. In Iceland and on hot spots like the Hawaiian Islands their presence is spectacular and obvious but not usually dangerous. However, when the earth's crustal plates meet head on and one plate overrides another, a more potent brew of magma fights to the surface.

The magma chambers below Tongariro National Park contain a hybrid brew of basalt, wet seafloor sediments and gases. This concoction also mixes with overlying mantle and crustal material on its rise into the magma chambers. It may also remain in these chambers for some time allowing minerals to crystalize and the liquid to change composition. The upshot is a lava richer in silica than basalt and consequently stickier. This lava produces volcanoes of an intermediate type called andesitic volcanoes. In some instances these stiffer lavas emerge from craters as lava flows, like those which issued from Ngauruhoe in 1949 and 1954. On other occasions the lava is blown to pieces in the volcanic vent and spread far and wide as ash, as happened on Ruapehu in 1945. A combination of these two types of andesitic eruption has built up the volcanic cones, ash deposits and lava flows which form the landscape of the park today.

The really big events, however, occur when lava called rhyolite is formed. Rhyolite is so rich in silica (over 66%) and consequently so stiff, that it clogs normal vents sealing in the gases. Enormous volumes of gas build up and when the top finally blows all hell breaks loose. The last time this occurred in New Zealand was about AD 186, long before either Maori or European set foot in the land.

In this catastrophic eruption the earth around Taupo bulged and ripped apart, loosening an enormous column of fine ash. The volcanic plug which had previously kept the lid on the underlying gas-saturated magma was blown to pieces, the heavens were rent apart, and the sky darkened in the pall of a mushroom cloud which rained down rocks and ash for hundreds of kilometres downwind to the east. Then, in a slow-motion movement, some of the towering column subsided, falling back in on itself. A fireball avalanche of pumice sped across the landscape at hundreds of kilometres per hour, a firestorm armageddon, filling river valleys and incinerating all life in its path over an 80-km circle. Pumice from that explosion is found on Tongariro and at Iwikau ski village on Ruapehu 1000 m above the level of Lake Taupo. Charcoals are common in these pumice deposits testifying to the fact

The flat summit of Tongariro's North Crater was possibly once a lake of molten lava, whose encircling crater rim has eroded away. The smaller crater, which is about 300 m wide is a more recent explosion pit.

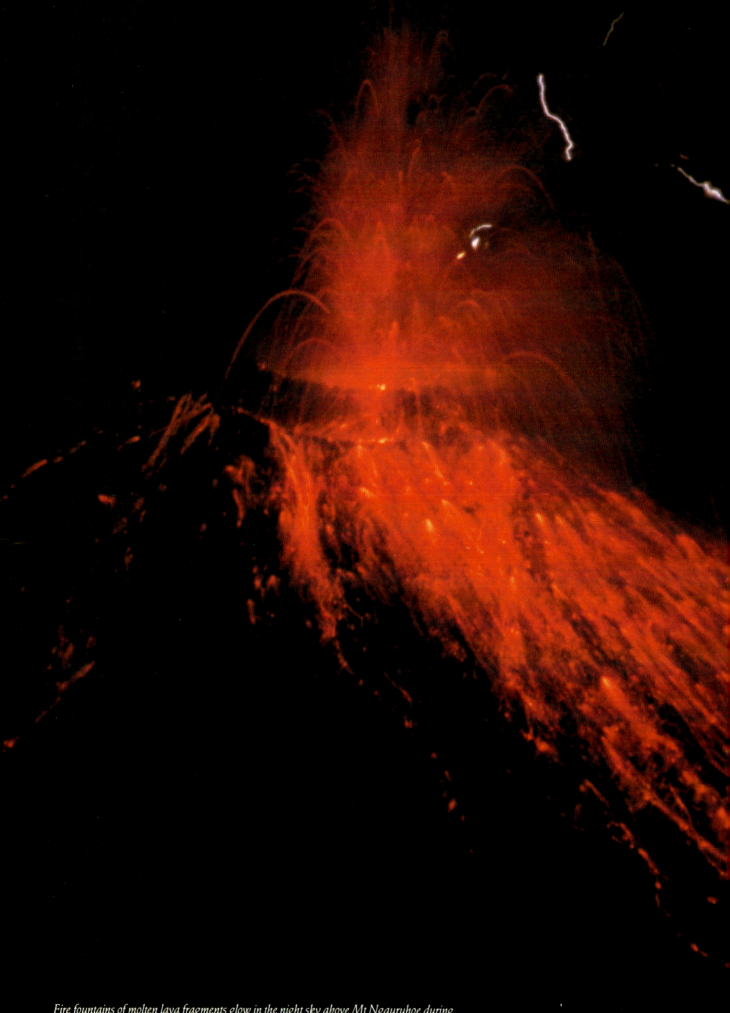

Fire fountains of molten lava fragments glow in the night sky above Mt Ngauruhoe during the 1954 eruptions. The bright streaks are caused by static electricity.

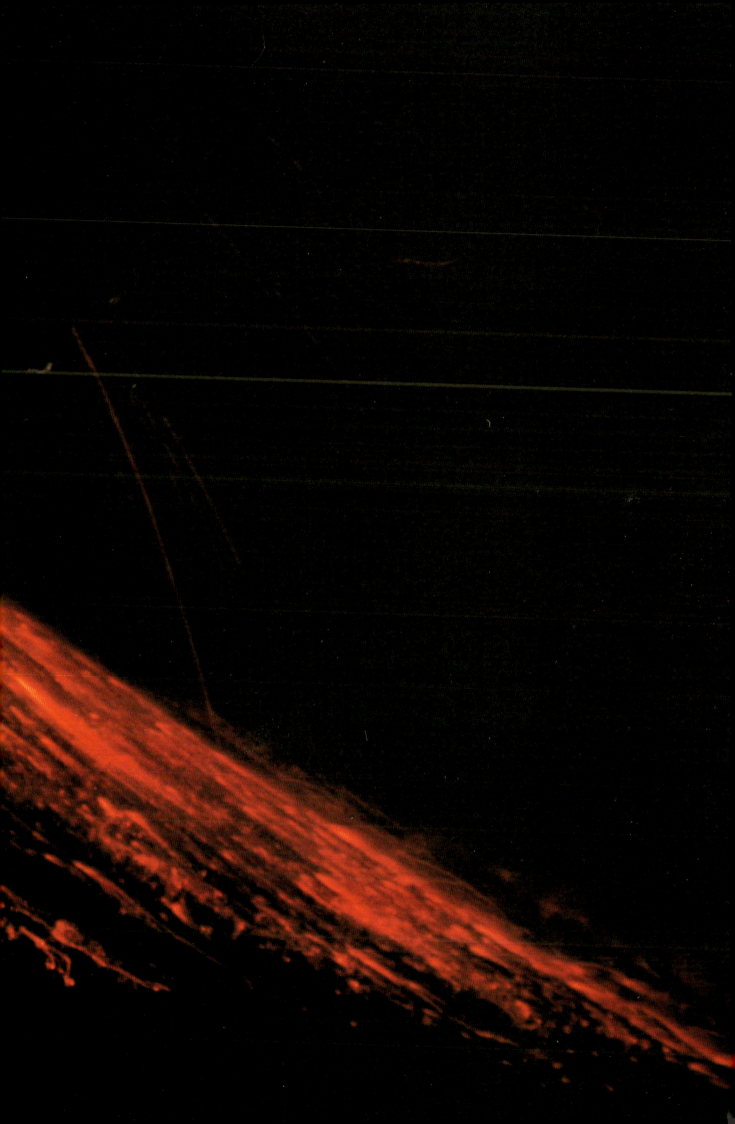

that in a few fate-filled minutes approximately two thirds of the flora and fauna of the park were wiped out. This event is believed to have deposited upwards of 110 km³ of new material on the earth's crust. In the aftermath of the violent explosions the land in the immediate vicinity sank to form a basin-like depression (or caldera) which is now the northeast arm of Lake Taupo.

Trees incinerated by this Taupo eruption have been radiocarbon dated at between AD 130 and 200. But it is also possible that the effects were seen and recorded in the northern hemisphere. Hou Han Shui, a Chinese court historian recorded that:

> During the reign of the [emperor] Ling Ti (AD 168-189) several times the sun rose in the east as red as blood and lacking light; only when it had risen to an elevation of more than two zhang (24 degrees) was there any brightness. When it set in the west at two zhang above the horizon it was similarly red... Also during this period several times when the moon rose and set and was two or three zhang above the horizon all was red as blood...

The Roman historian Herodian also reported strange events.

> Stars were seen all the day long and that some did stretch in length hanging as it were in the midst of the air which was a token of a cloud not kindled but drawn together, for it seemed kindled in the night...

And another Roman source (Scriptores Historiae Augustae) mentioned that: 'Before the war of the deserter (autumn AD 186) the heavens were ablaze...'

How can we be sure that these descriptions refer to the Taupo eruption? Simply because there is no geological evidence of a large volcanic event anywhere else in the world at this time, and the descriptions are remarkably similar to those received all over the world after the Krakatoa eruption in Indonesia in 1863. This eruption, which killed 36,000 people in its accompanying tidal wave, was somewhere between one quarter and one sixth the size of the Taupo event. The dust and clouds from Krakatoa rose 80 km into the sky and the blast was heard some 5000 km away in Australia. In both cases there seems little doubt that the dust penetrated the upper stratosphere and would have taken years to fall to lower levels again. After Krakatoa, weird red sunsets were described and painted in Europe for two years and the climate was noticeably cooler, both seemingly the result of Krakatoa's volcanic dust blocking the rays of the sun.

Awesome as it must have been, the Taupo eruption of AD 186 had been preceded by very much larger events. Eruptions appear to have occurred in the Taupo-Rotorua region which boggle the mind in their enormity. Ash deposits have been found far out in the Pacific Ocean and scientists are forced to conclude that something in the order of 1000 km³ of ash were spread over an area of 30 km² by a single volcanic event about 300,000 years ago. By comparison, Krakatoa ejected 18 km³ in 1883 and Mt St Helens a mere 1 km³ in 1980. Indeed this earlier Taupo eruption is thought to have been one of the largest in the world in the last one million years, and a sudden dip in the earth's atmospheric temperatures after the event may have been caused by a volcanic dust fallout which created conditions similar to a nuclear winter. Just 20,000 years ago an eruption ten times larger than that in AD 186 occurred, and events of this magnitude appear to have happened at a rate of about one in every 30,000 years in the Taupo region throughout the past one million years.

Although the present national park landscape is largely the result of eruptions on Tongariro, Ruapehu and the neighbouring volcanoes, the much more violent Taupo volcanic events have had a far greater influence on the plants and animals of the park. Throughout the park evidence of the last great eruption from Lake Taupo is preserved in the charcoal laden pumice layers. Only on the western and southern slopes of Ruapehu are there large areas of vegetation which have escaped untouched, except by more gentle falls of wind-whirled ash.

Charred wood from trees incinerated during the AD 186 Taupo eruption is spread in the white pumice throughout the park. In less than 30 minutes, approximately two thirds of the park's vegetation was destroyed.

Part of the crater wall enclosing Mt Ruapehu's Crater Lake.

STRATO-VOLCANOES

With the major exception of the Taupo pumice layers and the odd outcrop of sedimentary basement rock, the geology of the park is totally dominated by the andesitic volcanoes of Mts Kakaramea, Pihanga, Tongariro-Ngauruhoe and Ruapehu. These mountains are all 'strato-volcanoes', a term indicating that they are composite cones built up of alternating beds (or strata) of ash and scoria which have fallen out of the sky, and intervening bands of lava which have flowed down the mountainsides. The lava flows have also strengthened the whole formation by partially protecting the softer ash and scoria beds from erosion.

Virtually all these volcanoes and their respective vents lie in a straight line. This runs more or less northeast to southwest, and suggests that the magma chambers which periodically feed the various cones are aligned along a fracture or narrow zone of fissures. Moreover, this alignment of active volcanism is paralleled by a series of faultlines, strongly implying that the line of vents is the result of recent tectonic movement. Where vents such as Pukeonake, Kakaramea and Tihia are at odds with this general pattern it seems probable that they are aligned along stress faults lying at right angles to the main system of faultlines.

Active strato-volcanoes are often very complex structures made up of a series of unrelated eruptions which tend to obliterate, or at least overlay, the evidence of earlier volcanic activity. On both Tongariro and Ruapehu there is little regularity about the dates of the various eruptions or their type and intensity, and accordingly it is very difficult to describe their past and present features as an orderly sequence of events. In some respects, therefore, the rest of this chapter is of necessity a little like the landscape itself—somewhat of a chaotic jumble, but I hope always full of interest and surprise.

Tongariro is probably the oldest of the park's volcanoes. Lava flows associated with the Tama Lakes area date back 261,000 years, but it is conceivable that volcanic action began over 500,000 years ago, with the outpourings of earlier eruptive phases now lying deeply buried beneath more recent layers of lava and ash. Today Tongariro stands like a colourful old warrior, battle-scarred and ragged. Its sprawling battledress has jewels of small emerald lakes, blood-red rocks, and splashes of silver and yellow to contrast with its more dominant greys and blacks. Recent adolescent outbursts like Ngauruhoe and Red Crater, on Tongariro, ride over the old order, but it is reasonable to picture a young Tongariro rivalling Ruapehu in height. Even in middle age, when wooing a young and beautiful Pihanga (as in the Maori legend), Tongariro would have commanded centre stage, successfully banishing the other volcanoes to the wings. The massive walls of the Mangatepopo and Waihohonu valleys, and side-vents such as Pukekaikiore, suggest that a large volcano existed somewhere near the site now occupied by the youthful cone of Ngauruhoe. However, deep erosion, especially during the many ice ages, and numerous explosive eruptions have wrecked the internal structure of this older order.

After erosion of this older Tongariro new vents burst forth in the last glacial and post-glacial periods. The oldest of these eruptions was North Crater, which fired into action over 50,000 years ago, periodically sending out lava flows and spraying tephra (ash and other material blown out during eruptions) across the landscape. This crater remained active in post-glacial times until its lava began to cool and solidify. A dying burst of gas later erupted through the congealing lake to create a small explosion pit in the northwest corner. Alongside North Crater, lava was also splattered from fire fountains in the vicinity of today's Blue Lake about 9700 years ago. During this same period at least a further six explosion craters were active, including the Tama Lakes in the south, which erupted up through the most ancient lava to have been dated in the park.

At the centre of Tongariro, Red Crater presents a weird, cloven shape, its form almost sexual in connotation, streaked in blood-red and steel-grey scoria, and often spotted by incongruous drops of pure white snow. Numerous times in the past 10,000 years Red Crater has spurted clinkery 'aa' lava (a Hawaiian term denoting the rough surface of these

Although very young the volcanoes of Tongariro National Park are the successors of a large family of volcanoes which have intermittently exploded onto the New Zealand landscape over the last 500-600 million years. In this photograph the snow-streaked Mt Ruapehu and the young perfect cone of Mt Ngauruhoe rise above the Red Crater with its Emerald Lakes and recent black lava flow. In the foreground is the explosion crater containing Blue Lake.

Volcanic tephra and lava are readily converted to clays by thermal activity, creating this maleable and colourful material at Ketetahi.

A 15-m thick, black andesitic lava flow poured from the upper Te Maari region 450 years ago.

lava flows which have cooled to jagged solids while the interior of the floor was still moving) into the Outere Valley, Central Crater and South Crater. One eruption in particular left a unique signature. In this event lava rose to the surface as a vertical sheet (dike) and poured from the fissure as a rapid flow. Later, when the magma chamber lost pressure, the remaining lava in the dike oozed back down leaving a striking vertical cavern in the crater wall. Five relatively large lava flows post-date the AD 186 Taupo eruption. The most recent explosions of Red Crater have been in 1855 and 1926, and today steam continues to rise from the main crater as well as discharging into the parasitic pit craters known as the Emerald Lakes.

If Red Crater conjures up images of a violent and wildly expressionistic character, then the Maari Craters on the northern slopes of Tongariro are perhaps the more classical and composed counterparts. They convey a soft serenity that cloaks their violent origins. Despite its almost perfect form, which suggests a very youthful volcano, the lower crater probably began to erupt about 14,000 years ago. More recent activity in these parts all appears to have come from the site of the upper crater. About 450 years ago a vent in this region sent a massive 15 m-thick tongue of lava flowing into the forests below Ketetahi. The present form of the crater, however, dates from eruptions in 1868. It also erupted in 1892 and again in 1896-97 showering ash to a depth of 50 mm on to the Desert Road. Throughout this century Te Maari has continued to fume away from steam vents on the crater walls without any further major eruptions.

Probably the kind of event which has produced much of the present Tongariro landscape is described in the following account from John Chase, who witnessed the eruption of the upper Te Maari crater on 30 November 1892:

> After a few preliminary shocks and rumblings, Te Mari...belched forth an immense quantity of steam, mud and boulders in a terrific manner. The stuff ejected rose 2000 or 3000 feet in the air and fell in the vicinity; thence it came rushing down the mountainside, scorching up trees on its way. It was a pretty sight to see the huge mass pouring down from the crater until it was lost sight of in the bush; thence it emerged two miles further down, divided into several small streams, looking in the distance like a number of mobs of sheep. The mass came rolling down the mountainside and fell on to the dray road near Rotoaira Lake.

At 2797 m Ruapehu is the highest mountain in the North Island, and has evolved in a manner just as complex and tangled as Tongariro. Several hundred thousand years of andesitic eruptions from numerous vents have built up the present summit massif. Pinnacle Ridge provides its oldest dated rocks, and these are thought to be the vertebrae of an ancient volcano which was active about 230,000 years ago. Erosion of this ridge has pared back the interior of the cone of this lost volcano to reveal central magma bodies which never managed to reach the surface, and have been altered to a deep orange colour by circulating hot water.

Changes in the location of the main summit vents have provided the long complex of plateaux and ridges which make up the present crest of Ruapehu. Later eruptions and long periods of subjection to the relentless grind of moving icefields have combined to erode and reform the earlier eruptive centres. Lava flows are known to have poured through ice-filled valleys from the northern summit region between 14,000 and 10,000 years ago, reaching as far as the Silica Springs and laying the giant lava steps which now extend back up the Whakapapa slopes. Lava also appears to have erupted between 10,000 and 5000 years ago from small parasitic vents, including the one on the northern side of the mountain which sent lava flowing towards the Tama Lakes. Interspersed with these lava outpourings were a series of ash eruptions. These built up layers of tephra (unconsolidated airborne material) between the lava bands are usually thicker on the eastern side of the mountain because of the prevailing westerly winds. In the last few thousand years the main centre of eruptive action has moved southwest, into the region of the present Crater Lake.

THE WOMB

Your fires burnt my forests
leaving only the charred bones
of totara rimu and kahikatea

Your ploughs like the fingernails
of a woman scarred my face
It seems I became a domestic giant

But in death
you settlers and farmers
return to me
and I suck on your bodies
as if they are lollipops

I am the land
the womb of life and death
Ruamoko the unborn God
rumbles within me
and the fires of Ruapehu still live

Apirana Taylor

Between Tongariro and Ruapehu the high cone of Ngauruhoe (2291 m) is one of the world's most active volcanoes, erupting at intervals of between two and seven years. Yet despite its spectacular displays it does not represent the same threat to human life and property as a potential Taupo explosion or even a major lahar flow (see next section) on Ruapehu. Its classical volcanic form has been created in only the last 2000 years by a series of generally contained eruptions, comprising the typical andestic pattern of alternating explosive ash showers and slow, sticky flows of 'aa' lava.

The most recent of the lava eruptions on Ngauruhoe was in 1954, when a series of flows rolled and steamed down the western flanks of the mountain into the Mangetepopo Valley, accompanied by ash showers and strombolian fountains of lava. In the words of eye-witness geologist Donald Gregg:

> The more rapidly moving parts of the flow were moving forward bodily. Boulders were tumbling from the face and exposing the red-hot interior of the flow as it slowly advanced over the fallen debris. As blocks fell off incandescent dust trickled out. The finer dust particles remained suspended in the air, producing a reddish-brown smoke most irritating to the eyes. As the flow moved it produced continual grating and clanking noises. There was no strong smell apart from a typical 'foundry odour'.

During this eruption approximately 10,000,000 m^3 of magma were ejected as lava flows, some of which are more than 18 m in depth.

In January and March 1974, and February 1975, Ngauruhoe performed again, sending towering columns of ash-laden gases up to 9 km into the sky. On several occasions the volume of debris in the rising column became so great that an avalanche of blocks and ash rained down on to the northwestern slopes. These explosive eruptions were accompanied by strong volcanic earthquakes, visible atmospheric shock-waves, and loud detonations.

Nothing is more certain than that Ngauruhoe will erupt again and again in our own lifetime. But the full extent of the power of the magma bodies beneath us will only really become apparent should Taupo happen to reawaken from its slumber.

'From the Dome, we look into the eye of the beast, where the blinding whiteness of the glacier ends abruptly at an abyss filled with tepid grey water. In the midst of such a forbidding landscape, it is clear that we must meet the volcano on its own terms. The colour of Ruapehu's eye depends on its moods, which can change rapidly and with little warning. During temperamental spells, it is a muddy grey, while cool tranquillity is reflected by deep blues and greens. The lake is a natural laboratory where minerals grow from solution and settle out, producing a bottom layer of grey mud. The mud plays an important part in affecting the behaviour of the lake, since it forms a barrier between the water and the magma which seethes below. If the fragile mud barrier is disrupted, water and magma may come into catastrophic contact, instantly producing large volumes of superheated steam.'
Bruce Houghton, geologist

According to a Tuwharetoa tribal myth, the pulsating heart of Maui's fish (New Zealand's North Island) is Lake Taupo. Taupo eruptions have been amongst the largest and most devastating volcanic events on the planet during the last two million years. Lake Taupo itself is a series of collapsed caldera. In the midst of these hollows, plugs of low-gas magma have oozed to the surface as rhyolite domes which now form islands.

Oturere lava flows.

LAHARS

Not long after you turn off highway 47 on the way to the Chateau a series of distinctive mounds begin to dot the roadside. Over the years a number of explanations have been given as to how they may have formed. Some geologists have postulated that they are old moraines from huge ice age glaciers while others have suggested that they were small volcanic vents. Another intriguing explanation was that they were bubbles which formed when lava blistered as it flowed over a water-laden swamp. Today it is generally thought that they are graphic expressions of the extent of vast mudflows of volcanic debris known as lahars, a term coined by Dutch geologists to describe the eruption avalanches which occur on the rain-drenched volcanoes of Indonesia.

Lahars are triggered when volcanic material is converted into a mudflow by the addition of water, not only from heavy rain but also when an eruption occurs beneath a crater lake or in regions where large amounts of water are stored as snow and ice. The causes and effects of lahars have received very little attention until recently although they are among the most destructive consequences of volcanic events. Over 5000 people died when a river of mud from the Indonesian volcano Kelut rampaged through a village in 1919 and 25,000 perished in 1985 when Nevado del Ruiz erupted in Colombia.

In New Zealand lahars have killed more people than any other type of volcanic activity. At 10 pm on Christmas Eve 1953, a puzzled Cyril Ellis stopped his truck before the Whangaehu River bridge. In amazement he gazed through the light of the headlamps towards a raging river that engulfed the bridge making any chance of crossing it that night impossible. How was it that the river was in monstrous flood yet the day had been perfectly fine? Ellis had little time to ponder before he saw the Wellington – Auckland express train approaching the railway bridge a few hundred metres upstream. He rushed to the line and ran down it waving his light.

> ...it was no use – they just didn't see the torch. I jumped clear and yelled to the driver when the locomotive roared past me about 200 metres from the bridge, but he had no chance of hearing me above the roar of both river and engine.
>
> ...The train went straight on over the bridge. Halfway across, the engine simply nose-dived off the southern bank and seemed to go with a bellowing splash nearly against the opposite bank. The first carriage went with it. You never heard such a noise. It sounded as if the engine had exploded. The second carriage reared up, nose first, and with the weight of the carriages behind it was more or less catapulted into the air. Then I noticed three carriages following, which immediately seemed to break into three separate parts. They hit the water and I could see them floating down the river with the lights still on. After they had travelled about 40 metres they disappeared and I no longer saw their lights.

A stupefied Ellis watched as the locomotive and first five carriages plunged into the flood. The sixth carriage hovered on the brink at a 45 degree angle. Ellis raced forward and cried to the guard, William Inglis, to get the people out, and then climbed into the carriage himself:

> ...I did not have a chance to do anything whatever before the movement became more severe. The car rocked sideways slightly at first and then a little faster, and then at the same time the front of the car tilted downward but not to a great degree. I grabbed a seat and then the luggage rack to enable me to remain standing. A few people screamed, but I sang out 'Don't panic, don't panic. Hang onto the luggage racks'. By this time the water was pouring into the car and the lights had gone out. The rocking of the car continued together with a violent bouncing. I was at this time standing on the seat and the water was up to my armpits. The next I realised was a terrific bump and the car tipping on its side to the left. The coupling cracked and we all went over the brink. I still had my torch

The andesitic volcanoes of Tongariro National Park line up at the southern end of the Taupo volcanic zone. The perfectly shaped Te Maari Craters and Mt Tongariro's North Crater dominate the foreground, while the youthful cones of Mt Ngauruhoe and Mt Ruapehu stand behind.

in my hand and as we hit the water I was yelling to the people not to panic. It was as though we were spinning around in a barrel of water. As the carriage lights failed I gripped onto the luggage rack. She rolled over a couple of times and then came to rest on her side, with the water flowing through. It was wicked. I had a couple of women hanging on to me, but I managed to knock out a window with my elbow and kicked it with my shoe to enlarge the opening and break off the jagged pieces...

Ellis and a passenger John Holman pulled 26 others out through the broken window on to the top of the carriage where they crouched cold and wet for an hour before rescuers formed a human chain out from the bank. In the dark, raging river many fought for their lives, but 151 died. Twenty bodies were never found and it was presumed that they had been washed out to sea 120 km away. Tangiwai, the place of this tragedy, literally means 'weeping waters'.

During the inquiry into the cause of the Tangiwai disaster the New Zealand public learned of the highly destructive effects of what had been, up until then, a little known volcanic process – the lahar. Under a cloud of sorrow the inquiry methodically traced the sequence of events which led to the tragedy. These began eight years earlier with Ruapehu's only major eruption this century.

In early March 1945 small explosions had begun in the Crater Lake. These had been preceded by the growth of an island of steaming lava in the lake which had disintegrated from within, only to be replaced by a larger lava dome in May and June. Later, in August and September, violent explosions had rocked the Crater Lake shattering the dome and sending ash clouds high into the sky to settle as far away as Wanganui. By January 1946, pools of water had formed in the crater which had now been enlarged to a depth of about 300 m. By 1953, the lake level had stabilised about 8 m higher than preceding the 1945 eruptions.

What appeared to have happened was that the 1945 eruptions had caused ash and other volcanic debris to plug the old outlet of the lake. This barrier of ash, lava and ice gave way at about 8 pm on Christmas Eve 1953. As the lake level fell 6 m in the space of a couple of hours huge volumes of water careered off down the Whangaehu River picking up great quantities of loose ash and boulders on the way. A similar sudden escape of the Crater Lake waters had occurred in January 1925 when an ice cave had burst open and the Whangaehu River had risen three metres at Tangawai, also damaging the bridge carrying the Main Trunk Line.

Lahar flows much smaller in magnitude can also be dangerous on Ruapehu. Just after midnight on 22 June 1969 an explosion from the Crater Lake destroyed a shelter hut on the crater rim and created seething mudflows that snaked down the mountain at high speed, wrecking a kiosk on the skifield. Twelve hours previously, several thousand skiers had been scattered across these same slopes. Had the lahar occurred then, somewhere between 20 and 40 people would probably have lost their lives, and the death toll could have been as high as 100 if it had taken place during the August school holidays. These days, with far higher numbers congregating on the mountain, the potential for tragedy from these sudden volcanic mudflows is very real. As the official report on the 1969 lahar concluded: 'It is unlikely that it will ever be possible to predict and issue warnings of individual eruptions in specific form, though it may prove possible to predict some in general terms.' Still, the same kiosk hit in 1969 was caught again in a lahar flow in 1975, and this time, perhaps wisely, considered irreparable. Today a lahar warning system may give skiers 5-10 minutes to move to higher ground. But mountains like Ruapehu are time bombs which are constantly ticking away and there will always be some element of danger in playing on a live volcano.

In the past, huge lahar flows have cascaded from both Tongariro and Ruapehu, dwarfing those associated with recent volcanic activity. Perhaps at times the walls of crater lakes collapsed, or torrential rains lubricated the steep unstable slopes beyond the critical point. During the ice ages glowing debris of volcanic activity would have melted large quantities of ice and snow to produce a deadly mix, much as occurs in Iceland today when eruptions take place underneath the glaciers.

Over the centuries massive mudflows have poured out in all directions, creating the ring plains that completely surround Tongariro, Ruapehu and Kakaramea for 10-20 km. These thick slurries picked up huge quantities of ash and other debris, and, like glaciers, provided a momentum which was capable of transporting enormous boulders for many kilometres over relatively flat land. Some road cuttings surrounding the park thus reveal deposits which appear to resemble glacial moraines in their ill-assorted mixture of boulders and fine material. But these deposits have almost invariably come from lahar flows, the largest of which have flowed out across the flatter lands and reached as far away as Taumaranui and Taihape.

The sulphurous centre of the crater on Mt Ngauruhoe.

Lava fields from Red Crater contain huge ejected blocks which seem like ancient spiritual stones deliberately placed on an eerie wasteland.

Ketetahi hot springs are an obvious surface expression of heat derived from magma, near the earth's surface. Rainwater percolates down cracks and is heated to form steam which rushes back to the surface. These vents, fumeroles, may release gases up to 1000°C.

'Steaming soil, covered in every direction with yellow crystals of sulphur, and glistening silicous deposits'.

James Kerry Nicholls at Ketetahi, 1884

Tephra layers eroded by flash floods in the Rangipo Desert.

Taupo and Ngauruhoe ash banks up against an Oturere lava flow.

Lava spewed from a volcano remains plastic and glowing with heat for some time after exposure to the atmosphere. Sometimes it cracks in a striking fashion during the rapid contraction when the surface cools faster than the rock's interior.

ICE, WATER AND WIND

ICE, WATER AND WIND

Ice fingers raising soil.

On cold nights in all seasons of the year a quiet process occurs that is triggered only by a few degrees drop in temperature. Small droplets of water caught in between soil particles and rock crevices expand on freezing into delicate hairs and fingers of ice. From the sudden sublime power of volcanic explosions it may seem of trifling significance to focus closely on these small slivers of ice, which soon melt and flow to the sea. However, water, especially as ice, plays a major part in shaping the landscape of Tongariro National Park. With disjointed piles of loose ash and rocks dispersed among the harder lavas, volcanoes are extremely vulnerable to erosion. Still, erosion has its positive aspects, and in volcanic landscapes often creates the most exquisite and bizarre forms, reminiscent of the sculptor's hand rather than the everyday work of percolating water.

Every night in which water freezes on the mountains, processes called 'frost-heave' and 'freeze-thaw' lift and transport thousands of tonnes of loose dirt and small rocks. The water which freezes and expands breaks apart joints in the rocks into which it has seeped, and lifts particles of surface soil. As the ice melts in the morning the particles and fragments are pulled downslope by gravity along with the flow of water. The water collects as continuous trickles, the trickles become creeks, and the creeks grow into rivers (with beautiful Maori names) flowing radially from the peaks. Here on the sacred mountains two of the most spiritually-charged rivers in Aoteoroa begin – the Wanganui and the Waikato (or Tongariro). The headwater streams of these rivers gouge deep V-shaped gullies in the friable volcanic material, but walls of hard lava regularly provide greater resistance to their erosive powers and in such places waterfalls spurt as white cascades through dark bands of cliffs.

Although this erosion is happening continuously, the most striking visible signs usually occur swiftly during storms of great intensity such as those in March 1937 when 178 mm of rain fell overnight at the Chateau, or on 29-31 March 1945 when 220 mm fell in 46 hours. Many of the more obvious slips in the park can be dated from these and other catastrophic downpours.

Since the time of their earliest known activity Ruapehu, Tongariro, Pihanga and Kakaramea have been periodically torn at by glacial ice. Evidence of these periods of ice occupation is still shown in some of the park landforms including the U-shaped cirque basins such as the misnamed South Crater (it never was a single volcanic vent), arête peaks like Girdlestone, and rocks grooved and striated by the sandpaper effect of other rocks carried in the moving walls of ice. Evidence supporting large ancient ice masses can also be found at elevations as low as the Chateau. Straight U-shaped valley profiles and walls of moraine typical of former ice occupation are found in valleys such as the Mangetepopo, Wahianoa and Waihohonu, although lava flows in these valleys have possibly performed the same kind of land-shaping work as ice age glaciers.

Scientists are embroiled in debate about the bulk and extent of ice age glaciation in the park since much of the evidence has been obliterated by more recent volcanism. It is generally accepted that during the colder periods of the ice ages, when average temperatures were about 6°C cooler than today, the permanent snowline would probably have been 1000 m lower than at present and the vegetation of the park little more than stunted tundra forms, with the occasional resilient patch of beech trees and mountain toatoa. Such a barren landscape would have eroded very readily. Moreover, the mountains were heavily loaded with snow and ice and in eruptive events hot ash, mud, loose blocks and lava would have combined with melting water to create the lahar flows described in the previous chapter. These giant mudflows, lubricated by ice and snow, have piled successively onto each other to form the ring plains which now surround Ruapehu and Tongariro. They have also created the intriguing mounds which are now such an obvious landmark on the approach road to the Chateau.

All remaining vestiges of ice age glaciers have disappeared from Tongariro, but Ruapehu, with its greater height, still has seven small glaciers, none of which, however, is longer than 1 km. These are mostly confined to bowl-shaped cirque basins and for much of the year appear to be little more than residual snowfields. But they all have inner bodies of moving ice containing contorted crevasses which are usually exposed late in summer.

Compared to South Island glaciers the movement of ice on Ruapehu is slow. In 1951 a plane crashed on the Mangatoetoenui Glacier. Thirty-one years later wreckage from the crash emerged from the ice 500 m downslope. This isolated event indicates that the ice within this glacier is travelling at a speed of between 10 m and 20 m a year, which contrasts with 200 m a year on the Tasman Glacier at Mt Cook and up to 1800 m a year on the Franz Josef Glacier in Westland National Park.

As with most of the world's glaciers, the ice in Tongariro National Park has been steadily retreating throughout this century. The depth of ice in the Crater Basin Glacier has shrunk at a rate of 3 to 5 m a year over the past 30 years, and photographs taken in 1909 confirm that about the same rate of ice loss has been in progress from the beginning of the century. Similar photographic comparisons also indicate a dramatic retreat of the Mangaehuehu Glacier, some 800 m to 900 m up-valley, since the early 1900s. And a glacier that filled the upper slopes of the Whakapapanui catchment finally melted into extinction in the 1970s.

In midwinter when deep snowfalls blanket the mountains and waterfalls freeze into fluted pipes it is not difficult to imagine the glaciers descending towards the forests and tussock again. Indeed some climatologists believe that we may still be part of a continuing ice age and are at present enjoying a merely temporary warmer interlude before the inevitable return of chillier times.

Immediately following the last major glaciation which retreated rapidly from 14,000 to 11,000 years ago, erosion was at its most intense pre-human phase. The long period of colder temperatures had devastated the protective cloak of forest and when the great masses of glacial ice melted back, the steeper parts of the bare landscape rapidly collapsed. It has also been suggested that the release of pressure on the mountains brought about by this ice retreat allowed the magma bodies within the earth's crust to rise, leading to a period of increased volcanic eruptions from 14,000 to 9000 years ago.

An obvious effect of more recent glacial recession has been the creation of a dangerous rim of weak unsupported rock on the eastern edge of the Crater Lake. A sudden collapse of this rim could send a surge of hot water, mud and other volcanic debris (a lahar) down the Wangaehu River causing devastation equal in magnitude to the 1951 Tangiwai disaster. This instability is the direct result of the shrinking of the Crater Basin Glacier which has released pressure on the crater rim and caused the rock to loosen and rebound inwards.

Crater Lake outlet in winter.

Crater Lake glacier.

THE TURNING

The turn of water to ice
and green to white the hills,
where already they are making
men from snow —
numbing their hands to make a man
who'll smile the smile they put there,
and tomorrow will weep endless tears,
not understanding.

I always wanted to live where it snows
(the white blanket every little girl's dream),
and now, out of the blue,
this silent settling of white alarms me —
cold as a violin's echo, spent and sharp,
but magical in the making.

The process is slow, insidious,
a hoar frost, blunt and final,
would be kinder than this
dark turning of water to ice.

Lynn Davidson

Waitonga Falls.

Falls in Makatote River.

Apart from the work of water, wind is the next most erosive agent among the natural elements. Winds blow strong and long over the volcanoes and are commonly recorded at 30-60 knots with gusts of 80 knots. Westerlies funnel especially strongly off Ruapehu's eastern slopes having dropped most of their moisture on the western side of the mountain. On the Rangipo Desert to the east, wind and water have combined to cut into the accumulated ash flows as if slicing through a richly-layered cake, exposing multi-coloured tephra and leaving pedestalled islands of tussock and scrub. In places these monoliths of vegetation are several metres above the surrounding desert landscape.

Once the vegetation has been removed by volcanic firestorms, wind, rain or lowering of temperatures, erosion is far more active, and there is little doubt that these natural processes

have also been sped up radically by European and pre-European firing of the landscape and the introduction of stock and noxious animals. Factors like these last ones tend to load the concept of erosion with negative emotional and moral overtones, but these have to be seen in a wider context. For the most part erosion is an entirely natural and inevitable process which also has its positive aspects. Huge supplies of trace elements are transported from the volcanic cones to the lowlands, while at the same time providing exquisite sculptures in the mountain landscape. Even the devastating flash floods carve tephra layers into minute grand canyons spurting out gravel and ash fans, and exposing incongruous boulders which have rocketed intact from the throats of the volcanoes during violent eruptive sessions.

A WHITE GENTIAN

Remember Ruapehu,
that mountain, six months ago?
You sat in an alpine hut
sketching scoria, red
rusted outcrops in the snow.

I climbed some southern peak
and made up the sort of song
men climbing mountains sing:
how, no longer your lover,
I knew it was over.

I thought I'd try out my song
when I returned that evening
as though there were nothing wrong.
Instead I brought a flower down
smelling of the mountain.

     Sam Hunt

The cotton daisy Celmisia spectablis *is the most widespread and versatile of the celmisias.*

LIFE

The sun orchid Thelymitra longifolia.

Unless restrained by waterlogged soils, altitude or human destruction, most of New Zealand would be naturally forested. Fresh mineral surfaces for forests to colonise are usually produced by erosion resulting from heavy rainfalls, glacial fluctuations or meandering rivers. Strong winds can also flatten large areas of existing forests returning them to an early stage in the regeneration sequence. In Tongariro National Park all these processes are active but they are often overridden by fires and the production of new volcanic surfaces: ash, lava and lahar.

With this constant renewal and change volcanic regions continue to produce very haphazard landscapes. But what makes Tongariro National Park so distinctive is not only its active volcanoes. There is also, within a fairly compact area, a fascinating range of habitats and patterns of vegetation which have evolved on this dynamic but often perilous landscape.

One especially obvious result is that in many parts of the park forest is absent at altitudes where it could be expected to be found. Instead there are only tussocks, shrublands or desert – a low and at times sparse blanket of vegetation which helps emphasise the grandeur of the volcanoes by creating a feeling of vast open space. Those forests which are found in the park are often distributed in unusual patterns. In between are areas of desert with constantly shifting sands and little or no vegetation; regions of alpine bogs surrounded by lush herbfields; and recent lava flows which even when 40 years old still have only small lichens and mosses growing upon them.

Why are there so few forests? Most obviously because the landscape has been repeatedly burnt by fires, some lit by humans and some volcanic. But there is more to it than this. The park is part of a far greater landscape which 1800 years ago was devastated by one of the world's largest volcanic explosions – the huge rhyolitic blast of the Taupo eruption (see FIRE) which would have completely dwarfed more recent events at places like Krakatoa and Mt St Helens.

Further back still, the forests of this region would have receded from the great quantities of snow and ice which covered the peaks during the ice ages. Following the end of the last of the major ice ages there was still a long period of thousands of years when the climate of the central North Island was too cold and too dry for the forest to return, and during this time much of the region was a large expanse of windswept sand and tussock, much like the present Rangipo Desert. It was only with a further warming of the climate and easing of winds some 5000-6000 years ago that the forest edge began slowly to creep back up the sides of the mountains.

Ranunculus flowers on Tongariro's South Crater.

By the time of the Taupo eruption the vegetation of the mountains of Tongariro National Park would have looked much like the other mountains of New Zealand. The young, stubby cone of Ngauruhoe was largely bare of open vegetation, but all flanks of Ruapehu carried forests. Large, red and silver beech forests stretched east from Mangawhero Stream (which flows from the Turoa ski-field down through Ohakune) out across the massive Rangataua lava flow towards Waiouru and northwards towards the Desert Road and Kaimanawa Range. Similar forests also clothed the lower slopes of the Pihanga-Kakaramea massif to the north of Tongariro.

With increasing altitude on Ruapehu, Tongariro, Kakaramea and Pihanga mountain beech took over from the other beech species and extended upwards to what was then the highest treeline in New Zealand. Mountain beech would also have grown down the wet western sides of Tongariro and Ruapehu where waterlogged soils made conditions unsuitable for red and silver beech. The versatility of mountain beech and its ability to survive on the toughest of sites would also have seen it growing as much drier forest in the rain shadow on the eastern side of Ruapehu and Tongariro. At the other end of the spectrum of tolerance, tall mixed podocarp forest occupied the better sites on lower areas surrounding Tongariro, Kakaramea and Pihanga particularly from Lake Rotoaira to the mouth of the Tongariro River.

Like the forests, wildlife was also much richer throughout the region then than it is today. Huia, piopio (the extinct native thrush), saddlebacks, flightless wrens, stitchbirds, weka larger than kiwi, tuatara, giant weta, large carnivorous snails and native frogs were among the inhabitants of the forests. In the open country above the bushline and around Ngauruhoe, flightless takahe and kakapo along with native quail and geese grazed the tussocklands. And high overhead a giant eagle with a wingspan greater than a condor soared the thermals searching for prey.

Much of all this was lost one autumn day some 1800 years ago when the safety valve suddenly blew on Taupo and a devastating flow of hot gaseous pumice blasted 80 km out in all directions, laying waste nearly one third of the North Island in little over half an hour. Almost all of Tongariro National Park fell within its destructive onslaught. The pumice flow raced across the top of old Tongariro and completely covered the young Ngauruhoe (then a mere 700 years old). But parts of Ruapehu remained more or less intact with the pumice slurping off to the sides of the mountain before it could over-top the summit. Thus the alpine vegetation high on Ruapehu and the forests on its southern slopes were the only major areas of vegetation in the park to survive the Taupo cataclysm.

Revegetation of the huge area destroyed by the Taupo volcano began immediately after the eruption. But because of very large differences in the manner and speed of seed distribution, the podocarp forests had a real advantage over beech species in occupying the fresh soil which developed on the layers of Taupo pumice.

The podocarps or native conifers like rimu, totara, miro, matai, kahikatea and kaikawaka have a seed encased in a fruit which is eaten by forest birds such as the kokako, kaka, tui, pigeon and bellbird. The seed survives passage through the gut and can thus travel long distances before coming to earth in the bird's droppings. In comparable circumstances in historical times, podocarp seedlings have been recorded over 7 km from the nearest adult tree on fairly recent volcanic soils (a hundred years after the eruption of Mt Tarawera in 1886).

Beech species do not have anything like as effective a method of spreading their seed. Beech seed has no fleshy fruit to make it attractive for birds, and is only lightly winged for its weight so does not get blown very far by wind. The most effective way for beech seed to move any distance is for it to be carried down a flooded stream and left high and dry on the banks to germinate. Away from streams beech boundaries advance very slowly, probably somewhere between 100 m and 200 m per 100 years.

In circumstances like those following the Taupo eruption the podocarps clearly won the

A seepage pocket on a lava flow creates an alpine habitat for mosses, celmisias, droseras, euphrasias and other alpine plants.

Lichens colonising a rock surface.

Raoulia hookeri var. albosericea *forms silver mats in the pumice.*

Moss and lichen, rock and ash.

race. Today we find podocarp forest extending high up the slopes of Kakaramea and Pihanga, growing at altitudes which should be the sole preserve of beech. However, patches of silver, red and mountain beech form a bushline necklace above the podocarps on both Kakaramea and Pihanga. Because of the way beech seed disperses it is exceedingly difficult to believe that these beeches have managed to reach this spot from beyond the outer edges of the Taupo pumice flows. There are also patches of beech on the north-western side of Tongariro which are very difficult to explain in terms of normal beech dispersal.

A clue to these riddles may well have been discovered in the aftermath of the Mt St Helens eruption in May 1980. As in the Taupo eruption, at Mt St Helens hot gaseous pumice was blown forth at terrifying speed as soon as the pressure holding the hot magma was released. Only 2 km from the vent and directly in the path of the full volcanic blast and debris flow was a small, sharp, forested hill. At the height of the eruption this hill was covered by hundreds of metres of flowing pulverised rock, and above this still, hot pumice. Yet, when all the dust settled, there in the midst of the down-slope side was a small patch of standing trees. Miraculously, they had survived on the side away from the blast, somehow protected from the incredibly abrasive flow which had sandpapered the rest of the hill completely bare.

Further out from the Mt St Helens vent, the volcanic blast overtook the huge rock flow and completely destroyed forests in a manner very similar to Taupo. As spring arrived thousands of hectares of grey pumice did not stir — the heat of the pumice flows had penetrated the soil killing even deep dormant seeds. But here and there were a few pockets where living plants had managed to survive the blast and green forest seedlings reappeared. These were in sheltered spots in the lee of prominent hills, or where some late snow had remained at the time of the eruption. This story of survival also includes the fact that these seedlings were usually growing from the undersides of tree trunks which had clearly fallen at some time prior to the eruption. When these trees crashed to the forest floor they trapped seeds beneath their great rotting bulk, and it was this bulk which insulated the seeds from the heat of the pumice flow.

Some Tongariro seeds may similarly have survived the heat of the Taupo blast in a few places not heavily covered with pumice, such as the southern (lee) side of Kakaramea and in some steep gullies stretching out from Tongariro towards the Kaimanawas. Thus small islands of seedling climax forest (that is, the kind of forest growing in these locations before the eruption) may have managed to maintain a foothold in a few scattered locations, surrounded by manuka and other shrubs which would have been the first to colonise the bare pumice. In 50 to 100 years these tiny forest patches were probably old enough to attract the larger seed-eating birds. And with the birds the podocarp seed would have returned from undamaged forest beyond the fringes of the great ring of destruction caused by the Taupo blast.

Before too long podocarp seedlings would have been growing up through the surrounding manuka, the beginnings of the great podocarp forests which since that time have dominated the central North Island, at least until the arrival of the axe and a new kind of fire. However, the process of re-establishment was not so rapid for some of the animals which had lived in the area before the eruption. Giant snails and native frogs, a couple of species of lizards and several flightless insects failed to recover their previous territory. Today they are found both to the north and south of the Taupo blast zone, but not within it.

And so to the next riddle. If the podocarp forest could be quickly 'flown' back in, and the unusual distribution of some of the present beech explained by the odd patch of seed surviving, then why is there so little forest on the western side of Tongariro, and between Tongariro and Ruapehu and the Kaimanawas? And why is the bushline on the northern side of Ruapehu only 1200 m to 1300 m? This is the warmer side of the mountain and normally the bushline would be expected to be highest here. But instead the highest bushline is formed by the ragged series of forest edges rising to 1540 m on the southern side.

The answer to this is found firstly in the growth of Ngauruhoe, Tongariro's youngest cone, and secondly, in the impact of humans who have lived in the area for hundreds of years. In both cases the main agent of forest suppression in areas where it ought to be growing today has been fire.

Two thirds of Ngauruhoe's young life has occurred since the Taupo eruption. The ash from the many intervening events can be clearly seen over-topping the Taupo deposits in places where profiles are exposed. But Ngauruhoe has not only erupted ash; there have also been frequent lava eruptions which have increased the height of the mountain considerably. These eruptions have also been responsible for starting natural fires in the forests surrounding both Tongariro and Ruapehu.

Especially in the drier eastern areas of the park, such fires destroyed the forests which had reoccupied the slopes of the active volcanoes. With each new fire tussock grasslands moved in to occupy the ground left by the burnt forests. And on the wind-swept summit of the pass between Waiouru and Turangi fires eventually led to the loss of even the tussocks, thus providing the beginnings of the Rangipo Desert.

Maori and European fires have further hindered the return of forests. The Maori used fire extensively throughout the central North Island, first probably to encourage the growth of bracken (for the staple food they made from its root), and later to clear land for kumara planting, to ease travel, and to assist in hunting kiore (the Polynesian rat, which was sometimes eaten).

When the first Europeans travelled through these parts the once extensive tall podocarp forests of the Kaiangaroa Plains had already been laid waste. Similar forests which had clothed the land surrounding Lake Taupo prior to the arrival of the Maori had been destroyed for several kilometres back into the surrounding hills. Some of the large tussock areas of the Kaimanawas and Kawekas are now also thought to have been created by deliberate Maori fires. And it is almost certain that the Maori assisted the work of nature in firing the forest on the slopes of the active volcanoes.

When the Reverend T.S.Grace arrived in the area in 1857 he thought that these extensive tussocklands would be ideal for sheep. Later, in 1874, his twin sons were involved in setting up the Kariori Company which by 1880 had almost 10,000 sheep grazing the Waimarino Plains, Rangipo and the northern parts of Tongariro. Accordingly, tussocklands in these regions were repeatedly burnt to encourage new growth. But the cost of transporting wool great distances, stock losses and 'bush sickness' led to the abandoning of the Kariori operation in the mid-1880s. Even though this was the end of grazing the tussocklands surrounding the park, fires were still used to aid the movement of stock through the region, particularly on the approaches to Tama Saddle between Ngauruhoe and Ruapehu. The problem of bush sickness arose from the lack of minute quantities of the trace element cobalt in the pumice soils, with the result that animals became thin and weak even though the pasture they were grazing appeared to be fresh and healthy. Although the Kaiangaroa Plains were otherwise seemingly excellent for grazing sheep, this cobalt deficiency was not discovered and corrected until after the Second World War. By this time however plantings in the 1920s and 1930s had covered these plains in pines.

Surprisingly Tongariro's first 'ranger' – or Honorary Caretaker as he was called – was himself responsible for many fires from 1912 until the 1920s. John Cullen was an Irishman who had a very different vision from most other people of the use which should be made of the park. He was a retired Commissioner of Police for the huge Auckland district and saw the park as a playground for his powerful and wealthy friends. In particular he envisioned a European-style sporting ground to which the rich could come to shoot introduced game birds.

It soon became clear that these views had very little popular support. Nonetheless,

An Olearia nummularifolia *shrub grasps the unstable tephra of the Rangipo Desert.*

Native tussock grasses dominate large areas of the park.

Cullen forged ahead with his plans to introduce heather to the park so that game birds such as grouse could be introduced. Heather seed was imported and Cullen set to work to get local nurseries to raise young plants for planting out and to grow others for seed production. The first heather was planted in 1912 and by 1917 over 15,000 seedlings had been planted and dozens of bags of seed broadcast over some 1200 hectares of the western part of the park.

All of this occurred against a background of very strong and well-informed public protest based on the fear that the introduced heather would displace the natural tussocklands in a national park. The Royal Society, various botanical groups, politicians, chambers of commerce, prominent citizens and major newspapers all complained about Cullen's high-handed actions. For his part Cullen had his circle of close friends and supporters, among them the then Prime Minister, the Rt Hon W.F. Massey.

Several times the issue was debated in Parliament. The standard of these debates was very high, with speakers from different parties showing a deep knowledge of the impact of introduced plants and animals on the unique New Zealand flora and fauna. Several predicted with great accuracy the likely results of introducing heather to the native tussocklands.

Probably realising that he would not be able to resist the public outcry for ever, Cullen tried several times to introduce grouse from Britain. Although it had been an easy job to import heather seed the birds proved much more difficult, and several consignments of wild pairs died while being shipped to New Zealand. Finally, in 1924, the SS *Rotorua* landed six live grouse in Wellington. The birds had been hand-reared by Lady Liverpool and sent to Cullen via his friend the Prime Minister.

If it had not been for a sharp reporter realising the significance of this particular cargo, Cullen might have got away with the introduction unnoticed. As it was, the arrival of live grouse was reported in the newspapers and a full debate in Parliament quickly followed. The result was that Cullen was forbidden to release the birds into the park, and the important principle that national parks should remain free from the introduction of alien plants and animals was finally established in law.

Many assumed that the matter would rest there. But if they did, they underestimated Cullen's stubbornness. He had the birds delivered to Waimarino (now called National Park) and history records that he obeyed the letter of the new law by releasing the birds on the other side of the road that formed the park boundary. Then, with a little bit of arm waving and shouting, the grouse were persuaded to fly across the road 'by themselves' and into the waiting expanses of heather.

For all his efforts and subterfuge this introduction was unsuccessful as Lady Liverpool's grouse failed to establish. But the episode had other consequences. Public pressure over the issue led to the appointment of a new Tongariro National Park Board which in 1925 passed a resolution that the heather should be eradicated. Not surprisingly the Honorary Caretaker made no attempt to carry out the orders of the Board. This inaction led to a situation where the presence of the heather was gradually accepted, most people simply hoping that it would not spread and become a major menace. Unfortunately, that is exactly what it has done, and today it covers huge areas of the park's tussock grasslands and threatens to destroy similar tussocklands in the nearby Kaimanawas and Kawekas.

The heather has little trouble in breaking the dominance of the native red tussock, growing up from underneath to eventually over-top and smother it. At the turn of the century the lower slopes of Ruapehu and Tongariro were golden with waving tussocks up to 2 m tall. Today these same slopes are mauve with heather.

This invasion by heather provides a new element in the natural struggle between tussock and forest, clearly to the advantage of the latter. Having over-topped the tussock the heather continues to grow and age, eventually becoming spindly and open. When it reaches this stage native shrubs such as mountain toatoa, hebes, coprosmas and five-finger become established.

Tussocks in Ketetahi Stream.

This heralds the beginning of a new forest – one which will be like the few remnant podocarp forest patches which still survive on the western slopes of Tongariro. Thus the park will eventually regain some of its forest cover. However, next time a volcanic eruption ignites a natural fire the park will not see a long period of open tussock grassland, but a more rapid succession back to forest. In this respect the ecology of Tongariro National Park will, unfortunately, never be the same again.

Heather is a threat not only to the lower tussocklands but also to the subalpine and alpine herbfields and regions of open gravels. On both Tongariro and Ruapehu heather has been found growing as high as 1600 m, and although at this altitude the plants appear to be infertile they can still be a problem. With this massive seed source close by (downslope to be sure, but also downwind) heather will continue to establish through these higher altitude regions. And even though infertile, the plants are still capable of growing and spreading sideways, thus smothering the subalpine and alpine herbs.

Another major problem weed introduced to the tussock grasslands and subalpine and alpine zones is *Pinus contorta*, a pine which often forms the treeline at about 3000 m on North American mountain ranges such as the Sierra Nevada. This pine was first introduced to the region by the New Zealand Forest Service in 1927, not long after the debate on heather had reached its climax.

These pines were planted in Kariori State Forest, low on the open, drier, south-eastern slopes of Ruapehu. The seed quickly spread up the mountain and was also blown considerable distances into the Rangipo Desert region, most of which is Army land. This self-seeding was so prolific that many square kilometres of dense pine forest were created, and all the Forest Service had to do was bulldoze the roads and fire-breaks. *Pinus contorta* unfortunately showed no respect for the boundaries between state forest and national park, or the treelines attained by native species. The inevitable consequence was that dense thickets of *Pinus contorta* began to appear in the park, many of them close to or above the natural treeline.

Concern by scientists, park staff and the Park Board about the spread of *Pinus contorta* began in the 1950s but was ignored by both the Forest Service and the Army. From the 1960s work by both park staff and volunteers managed to keep these pines at bay inside the park, but it was clear that unless the main seed sources on Forest Service and Army land were also eradicated there would be no end to the hard effort.

Where reason failed self-interest finally tipped the balance. The Army eventually realised that the pines were growing so fast and so thickly that they could no longer drive their tanks where they wanted to, and the defence of the nation rather than ecological principles demanded that they be removed. About the same time the Forest Service discovered that the wood was of little value for the recently constructed pulp mill at Kariori and accordingly the trees would have to be removed so that the land could be planted in much more suitable *Pinus radiata*.

With this change of heart from its two most important neighbouring landowners, Tongariro National Park sought to have *Pinus contorta* declared a noxious weed within 15 km of the park boundary, and hundreds of thousands of dollars have since been spent on its control.

The ability of both *Pinus contorta* and heather to survive the harsh conditions above the natural beech forest treeline poses a continuing threat to the alpine and subalpine vegetation of the region. As in other mountainous parts of the country the evolution of this vegetation is very unusual. But here the difficulties faced by all alpine plants are further compounded by the presence of active volcanoes.

Throughout much of New Zealand's geological history the country has been a group of relatively warm low-lying islands, with little in the way of mountains or regions of higher altitudes. The massive earth movements which have given rise to the present greywacke mountain backbone of New Zealand from Fiordland to East Cape are very recent, at least in

Introduced heather casts a purple haze over the yellow tussocks on the slopes around the eruption cone of Pukeonake.

Dracophyllum recurvum *is confined to the central and eastern mountains of the North Island.*

geological terms. Much of the uplift has occurred in the last two million years, a period which has also witnessed a considerable cooling in temperatures with the extensive areas of snow and glacier ice of the Ice Ages. In other words, in terms of both topography and climate, alpine environments are very recent arrivals in New Zealand.

If an alpine seedling is lucky enough to get itself successfully established it has to survive the other rigours of this habitat. Even on a clear day the air temperature at 1750 m will be several degrees lower than it is below the bushline at 1250 m. The problem faced by alpine plants therefore is how to make the most efficient use of the sun's energy to convert water and carbon dioxide into the sugars they need for growth.

Alpine species have evolved several different methods of dealing with this problem. One way is to trap still air next to the leaves so that it can be warmed. This is often achieved by covering the leaves with a thick coat of hairs, as the woolly daisy *Celmisia incana* does. Another is by evolving low prostrate forms, taking advantage of the warmer temperatures close to the ground and trapping air with low tangles of branches and leaves. Many alpines develop as mats or cushions which enables them to escape the worst of the winds and also to retain moisture during dry periods.

If a plant has any kind of height in this environment it needs to be particularly tough to withstand the strong winds and the abrasive effects of wind-carried sand and grit. Some shrubs like the golden *Olearia nummularifolia* have very thick, small, hard leaves and strong, heavy trunks and branches. Others, like whipcord hebes and pygmy pine, have very small, thick leaves that are closely pressed to a flexible stem.

Often alpine plants are seen growing most vigorously on sunny, north-facing slopes, or in the shelter of large rocks. The dark volcanic colour of these rocks helps them to store the sun's heat and therefore to warm their immediate surroundings.

All three volcanoes in the park have erupted intermittently since the Taupo event 1800 years ago, but, unlike their lava flows, their andesitic ash-fall eruptions have seldom caused extensive damage to the park's vegetation. Even though in places the ash fallout from significant eruptions has built up gradually to a depth of a metre or so, the high rainfall that the park experiences usually sees that these new soils are rapidly weathered.

Wherever there are changes in texture at particular depths (such as where the sandy Ngauruhoe ash overtops the coarser Taupo pumice) the weathered clays collect to form a layer that restricts the percolation of ground water. For this reason there are extensive areas of poorly-drained soils and bogs in the park, like those between Whakapapa Village and Hauhangatahi. These are dominated by red tussock, wire rush and *Glichenia* fern, and provide excellent habitat for other bog plants like the insect-eating sundews, dwarf ferns and several species of native orchid. These boggy areas are also the home of the elusive fern bird.

Immediately north of Hauhangatahi is the Waimarino swamp with the main road from National Park township forming its upper boundary. The presence of flax indicates that this wet area is more fertile than many of the bogs in the park, and provides an important seasonal food for bellbirds and tui. As the flax begins to flower hundreds of these birds gather from other parts of the park to drink the nectar at the base of the flowers, picking up the pollen as they do so and transferring it from plant to plant. The flax has evolved to meet this method of pollenisation by producing a tall and robust flower stalk which can support the weight of several large tui at a time.

This swamp creates a magnificent foreground for views of Ruapehu as you approach the park. On several of the slightly higher parts of it there are patches of mountain beech, again showing this tree's ability to colonise an environment which others find too difficult. The presence of beech on these higher locations has sometimes been seen as proof that the rest of this large basin is a swamp largely because of the poor local drainage. However vigorous regrowth at the edges of the beech stands, the presence of shrubs like five-finger and mountain toatoa amongst the flax, and the fact that the flax extends beyond the swamp up

The shifting sands of the Rangipo Desert.

The distinctive red strapped bark of kaikawaka, Librocedrus bidwillii.

Straight trunked kaikawakas penetrate kamahi and shrub understorey.

The insect-eating sundew, Drosera arcturi, *is common in bogs and in other areas of low fertility.*

Flowers of the mountain astelia.

Looper caterpillar on an astelia leaf.

The forest owl, Ruru or Morepork.

Toi toi grasses and coprosma.

An aged multi-trunked kamahi tree in the Makatote River gorge.

Cicada on tussock stem.

Mating native flies.

Leek orchid, Prasophyllum colensoi.

Native clematis.

Parasols of Coprinus *fungi growing on a mossy tree trunk.*

Lichen with spores.

Kawakawa leaves.

A forest underworld of ferns and seedlings.

Cyathodes sp. *bearing fruit and flower.*

Flowering mountain beech, Nothofagus solandri var. cliffortioides.

Toii or broad-leaved cabbage tree Cordyline indivisa.

Tall podocarp forest on the Pihanga Saddle.

An old buttress-rooted beech tree near Lake Rotopounamu. Since the AD 186 Taupo eruption which incinerated most of the park's forest, beech has been slow to recolonise old sites. Its seeds are not dispersed by birds and fly little distance beyond the parent tree. The presence of this ancient tree at Rotopounamu on the lee slope from the Taupo eruption suggests that such sites were surviving refugia and not recolonisations.

Whio, or blue duck, and chick at home in a mountain torrent.

North Island edelweiss, Leucogenes leontopodium

The sun orchid, Thelymitra decora, *flowers in early summer.*

A Burton Brothers portrait of the Tuwharetoa paramount chief, Te Heuheu (Horonuku) Tukino IV.

George French Angas — painter, writer, botanist and traveller — came to New Zealand for six months in 1844. He was befriended by the Tuwharetoa of the Taupo region and said of Te Heuheu (Mananui) Tukino II, 'his hair is snowy white and his people compare it to the snowy head of Tongariro; there being no object, except this tapu mountain, of equal sanctity to permit of its being mentioned in connection with the head of this chief'. Te Heuheu was killed in a landslip at Te Rapa two years after Angas' visit.

PEOPLE

THE GIFT OF TE HEUHEU

Te Heuheu Tukino IV, whose gift on behalf of the Tuwharetoa to all New Zealanders became the basis of the national park as we know it today, came from a long line of celebrated chiefs. We cannot appreciate him or his actions and the motives of his tribe unless we know something of his ancestors. In particular his father, Mananui Te Heuheu, whose spirit is bound closely with the park and whose bones strengthened the claim that his son made to the mountain at the time of the gift. History is usually told through the actions of those in power. For the Tuwharetoa tribe, who had lived beneath Tongariro for many hundreds of years, their main chiefs at the time of European contact were from the Te Heuheu family line. However, nearly all actions and decisions attributed to this great family were made on behalf of the whole tribe after lengthy discussions. From the times of Herea, who first heard of pakeha, to Sir Hepi, today, they speak not for themselves alone but for their people.

Te Heuheu Tukino II, the son of Herea, became paramount chief in the 1820s because he showed a natural ability to rally and lead the Ngati Tuwharetoa when they first came under pressure from northern tribes armed with muskets. Faced with the devastating power of the musket, Te Heuheu realised that if the more isolated Tuwharetoa people were to defend their lands and retain their mana they also had to acquire the deadly European weapons. Accordingly he arranged for a large quantity of flax to be prepared which he took to Maketu. There, he exchanged it for guns and ammunition with the coastal trader, Hans Tapsell. It was by showing strong leadership in actions like this that Te Heuheu acquired his mana, which was not simply assumed or inherited, even though his mother was a Ngati Maniopoto chieftainess and greatly respected by that powerful tribe. Te Heuheu was eventually proclaimed paramount chief and became the most influential leader in the interior of the North Island.

Te Heuheu gained the title of Mananui ('great prestige') through transference of powers from his uncle Taipahau who was a tohunga. The old man was dying and called for a messenger to go and get Te Heuheu. When Te Heuheu arrived he realised that a ceremony was about to be performed.

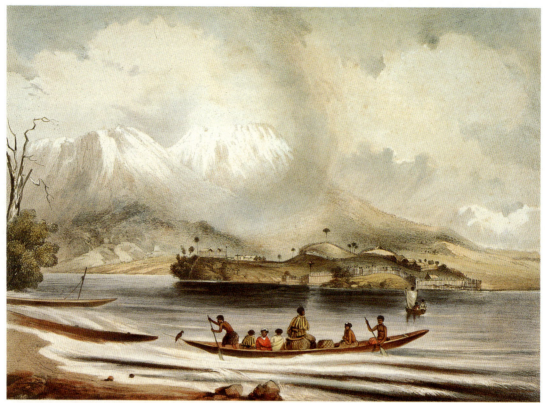

The Motuopuki Pa on Lake Rotoaira was as close as Angas was allowed to approach Mt Tongariro. Chief Te Heuheu (Mananui) 'gave me strictest injunction not even to look at the sacred mountain'.

The Motuopuki Pa, on a small island in the centre of the lake, features in tribal history. The lake also supplied an abundant food source of native fish and birds.

> Bending down he opened his mouth wide and closed it on Taipahau's right ear, and as he did so the old tohunga gave a few convulsive gasps and passed away. The ceremony was known as ngau taringa and...the powers of the old tohunga passed on to Te Heuheu...It was said that the old chief's spirit became his guardian and guide and his counsellor and protector during his battles.(Grace)

Mananui Te Heuheu lived at Te Rapa at the southern end of Lake Taupo with his eight wives (four of whom were sisters) in a strongly pallisaded pa. He was reputed to be a man of great physical and social stature, described by the early explorer John Bidwill as 'a remarkably fine man, upwards of six feet high, and very strongly built – a complete giant'. When Te Heuheu died Donald MacLean, a government agent, wrote in his journal:

> ...the very pride and boast of the New Zealand chieftains is now gone, nor will successive generations replace this with a more intelligent or well disposed man, well versed in every tradition and history of his country's people, as well as the productions of his country, of all of which, from the largest tree to the smallest shrub, he had some tradition or knowledge. He was a skillful botanist, and knew the physical uses of many herbs and plants. Nor was he ignorant of the insects and birds of the country...

While he was very hospitable and enjoyed the chance to discuss a wide range of subjects with visiting European travellers, Te Heuheu did not suffer fools gladly nor hesitate to put another point of view to the visitor. Cultural and political differences, philosophy and religion all came under the same stern scrutiny. Following a meeting with him at the Wanganui river in 1839 Edward Gibbon Wakefield wrote that:

> ...the old chief showed the most violent feeling of enmity towards the doctrine of the missionaries. Whenever he heard their followers sing one of their discordant hymns on our side, he would come out of his hut and muster one or two hundred to drown the sound by a native song.

As in the Motuopuki Pa painting with its dramatic and contrived clouds which are used to convey the sacred quality of the mountain, this painting by Angas of Tongariro and Ruapehu conveys a picturesque and unreal serenity to this wild landscape.

And in the words of historian James Cowan:

> The treaty of Waitangi has been signed by most of the principal men in the two islands. But one who steadfastly refused to set his mark to it was the greatest chief of all. This was Te Heuheu Tukino, the Ariki of the Taupo country...He declined with scorn the coaxing of the missionaries to become a Christian or to sign the treaty with the White Queen. 'I shall not abase myself by placing my head between the thighs of a woman...I am King here in Taupo...'

Mananui Te Heuheu met his death in May 1846 when a huge landslide broke away from the hill behind his pa and engulfed the buildings and sleeping inhabitants. The remains of the chief and his favourite wife were taken to Pukawa on Lake Taupo and placed in a vault there. A few years later Sir George Grey came with a party to Taupo, hoping to make an expedition up the mountains. A journal entry by G.S.Cooper takes up the story:

> Friday, January 4th, 1850. Whilst we were waiting for breakfast our attention was attracted by the most abominable howling, in the direction of the point, and on proceeding through the next enclosure we found that the noise emanated from the smaller yard beyond, in which were collected some thirty or forty people, in front of the fence containing the pataka...Raised on four legs, about two and a half feet from the ground, was a sort of box, about seven feet long by three and a half wide, covered with a blanket stretched in the shape of the roof of a house, so as to throw off the rain, and the whole painted with red ochre mixed with oil, blanket and all. The front, or side facing the pa, was fitted with hinges at the bottom and a fastening at the top, which, when unfastened, allowed the board to fall down like a flap, exposing the interior of the box. In it were the bodies of the late Te Heuheu and his wife, carefully wrapped in a handsome kaitaka mat, having been in this position for nearly two years and a half, but the pataka never having been opened until now, when it was done for the express purpose of

The pa at Otukou on the shores of Lake Rotoaira. Ketetahi springs fume on the slopes of Tongariro beyond the wharepuni. (meeting house).

The interior of Tapeka, a Ngati Tuwharetoa carved meeting house, at Waihi, on the shores of Lake Taupo. In their introductory booklet describing the carvings inside the meeting house, the Tuwharetoa state: 'The naming of the figures in the interior of the house was done so as to place the sub-tribal eponymous ancestors, and some of their descendants of the Lake Taupo district, on the left hand side on entering (Te Kopa-iti—the Place of the Host) and at the rear and the foot of the central pillar. The other figures on the right (Te Iho-nui—The Place of High Honour) are of ancestors from the tribes who inhabit the sea-board districts and the lands on the tribal boundaries and over the main water-shed ranges of Taupo-nui-Tia (The Great Taupo of Tia).

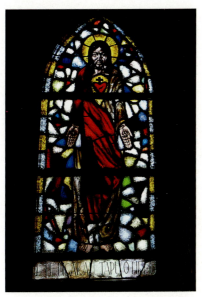  

Maori spirituality often involves a synthesis of Christian, ancestral and other traditional beliefs.

having a tangi preparatory to their removal to their final resting-place at the top of Tongariro.

The mountain burial was strongly opposed by Te Herekiekie, a neighbouring Tuwharetoa chief, who considered that such a burial would give force to a claim by the descendants of Te Heuheu to a mountain to which the Te Heuheu line did not have a sole right. Finally, however, the bones of the great chief were taken up secretly, and deposited on a ledge in a shallow cave about halfway up the northern slopes. A fierce storm broke out as the party was ascending the mountain. They believed this to be the work of enraged mountain gods, and decided to go no further.

A resolution of the tension created within the Tuwharetoa by the mountain burial was to come 60 years later. In 1910, in order to fulfil the terms of the gift of the mountain peaks as a national park, the remains of Mananui Te Heuheu were brought down from the mountain to be buried in a vault provided by the Government. The recovery party from Waihi had some difficulty in relocating the cave, but took guidance from a dream that the tohunga had had that a large fly would lead them. The next day, as a local musterer was having his lunch, he became distracted by the buzzing of a large blow-fly which, when he followed it, led him to the grave of the old chief. Later, when returning the bones to the foreshore of the lake, one of the carriers broke a law of tapu by jumping over a cooking fire which children had made. When he was returning with a party the following day a landslide came down in much the same area as Te Heuheu had lost his life and killed him.

Such was the power and mana of Mananui Te Heuheu. Potatau Te Wherowhero, who was married to Tuwharetoa chieftainess Ngawaero, visited Taupo before he was made King, and is reputed to have said: 'Ko Tongariro te maunga; ko Taupo te moana; ko Ngati Tuwharetoa te iwi; ko Te Heuheu te tangata.' ('Tongariro is the mountain; Taupo the sea; Tuwharetoa the tribe; Te Heuheu the man.')

Iwikau Te Heuheu assumed the role of paramount chief after the death of his brother. This was a time when the scale of social and cultural changes that were affecting the northern and coastal tribes were beginning to be felt in the more isolated inland areas. These changes included widespread social dislocation caused by pressure for land sales from the colonists, and an increase in disease and use of alcohol among the Maori. Then came the Land Wars.

On the 2nd of June 1858 Potatau Te Wherowhero of the Waikato Ngati Mahuta accepted Maori Kingship at Ngaruawahia. He headed an association of central North Island tribes wanting to stabilise internal Maori politics and reassert traditional Maori social control by preventing further sales of land to the colonists. The King movement involved the recognition that the Maori race itself must take positive steps to retain its identity in times of

Twice within a century the geologically unstable slopes of Kakaramea sent down devastating mudslides. Mananui Te Heuheu was killed by one in 1846 which was followed by a secret mountain burial of his remains. In 1910 the chief's remains were brought down from the mountain. One of the party on this expedition is purported to have broken a tapu and was engulfed in a landslide remarkably similar to that which had killed the chief.

change and also that a consolidation of their land base was essential to cultural survival. In the event, the Europeans over-reacted to a movement which was an intelligent and conservative response to change. The Land Wars followed, and the consequent confiscation of almost 2 million acres of 'rebel' land drove the King Party back into the Maniopoto territory.

Iwikau, who had been a great warrior in his youth, now adopted the role of peace-maker. In this he was influenced by his relationship with Thomas Samuel Grace, an Anglican minister, who came to the Taupo region with his wife and children in 1855 under the protection of Iwikau. Grace was an intelligent and practical man whose interpretation of injustices and deceit would be shared by many Maori people a century later. He held a view contrary to the predominant European fear in respect of the Maori King movement, and wrote in 1858 that he had

> ... not been able to discover anything hostile to British rule in the minds of the Maoris who desire a King, but rather that, by having a King, they will be imitating us. They also appear to think that through the medium of a King they may be able to check the present lawless state of things and to promote peace. The idea of anything like a rebellion, so far as I have seen, does not seem to have entered their minds, and they are not able to understand why such a step should give offence to us.

A marker post for the tapu Waihi landslide.

Grace also spoke out strongly against the unceasing efforts of the settlers and colonial Government to make the Maori sell their land.

> They find that, when they quarrel and fight and kill one another over the sale of lands, they are allowed to do so to their hearts' content, and have been officially told that the Government has nothing to do with these matters – in short, that they are not amenable to British law; but, as soon as a quarrel between themselves and the Europeans occurs, they are immediately said to be British subjects and denounced as rebels...The real cause of the war is, without doubt, the constant coercion that the Natives have been subject to in order to induce them to part with their lands.

Horonuku Te Heuheu, son of Mananui, became paramount chief on the death of his uncle Iwikau in 1862. He was bound by kinship to the Waikato people through his grandmother, with whom he was living at the time of his father's death. Thus Tuwharetoa warriors joined the battle at Orakau in 1864 when three hundred men, women and children held off 1800 British troops assisted by cavalry and artillery.

Orakau was one of the last major stands against the British and after this the loss of land accelerated. Whereas in the 1840s and 1850s the Government had dealt with sales on a tribal basis, after the Land Wars there was a move from tribal to individual sales. The *Native Land Act* of 1865 required the Native Land Court to individualise Maori land tenure, enabling persistent efforts of land-purchase agents, surveyors and prospectors to buy off individual Maori owners. The interior lands with their rich forests and farmland potential were the next area of expansion for an increasingly large immigrant population.

In an attempt to prevent further European encroachments through individual sales, the Tuwharetoa, as well as Rewi and Wahanui, two leading Maniopoto chiefs, decided to have their common tribal boundary defined. Because of the requirements of land legislation an investigation into the whole Taupo-nui-a-tia area was necessary, with a view to establishing the ownership of each individual block.

On 14 January 1886 the Maori Land Court began sitting before Judge Scannell at Tapuaeharuru (near the present Taupo) to determine the ownership of the vast territory known as Taupo-nui-a-tia according to Maori custom and usage. Hundreds of people attended the sittings which lasted many months. Chiefs from Te Arawa and Wanganui tribes, the Ngati Raukawa, Ngati Maniopoto, Ngati Kahungunu and from Taupo laid eloquent and often conflicting evidence before the court. Complex political changes had compounded long-standing inter-tribal jealousies.

For the first time the Tuwharetoa were having to confront the full significance of the European system of land law which was changing the entire basis of Maori land ownership. Traditionally, Maori tribal occupation, use and defence of an area ensured that members of a particular tribe held rights over that land. European law was to fragment this long-standing relationship by imposing concepts of individual title and rights.

During earlier gatherings and the Rangipo-murimotu hearing in 1881, the question of disposal of the mountains Tongariro, Ngauruhoe and Ruapehu had been debated. Horonuku Te Heuheu was being assisted in the proceedings by one of his sons-in-law, Lawrence Grace, the Member of Parliament for Tauranga and son of Thomas Grace, Iwikau's missionary friend at Taupo. In an adjournment during the hearings the elderly chief and his adviser went out onto the verandah where Horonuku asked:

> If our mountains of Tongariro are included in the blocks passed through the Court in the ordinary way, what will become of them? They will be cut up and perhaps sold, a piece going to one pakeha and a piece to another. Tongariro is my ancestor, my tupuna; it is my head; my mana centres round Tongariro; my father's bones lie there today. I cannot consent to the Court passing these mountains through in the ordinary way. After I am dead what will be their fate? What am I to do about them?

Lawrence Grace then raised the idea of making a gift of these lands to the Crown.

> Why not make them a tapu place of the Crown, a sacred place under the mana of the Queen? That is the only possible way in which to preserve them forever as places out of which no person shall make money...

'Yes', said the old chief, 'that is the best course, the right thing to do! They shall be a sacred place of the Crown, a gift forever from me and my people...

ACCEPTING THE GIFT

The events of 1886 took place at a time when the idea of parks belonging to the nation as a whole was beginning to gain acceptance in New Zealand from several different directions. Precedent for such parks had first been established in the United States where in 1864 the Yosemite Valley had been declared a 'State Park'. Then in 1872 land at the head of the Yellowstone River was declared a 'Nation's Park' with specific protection for flora, fauna and 'natural curiosities'.

Similar sentiments had also been emerging in colonial New Zealand, although not without spirited opposition. The Austrian geologist Ferdinand von Hochstetter who visited New Zealand in 1858-59, protested at the ransacking of the great Northland kauri forests 'for the sake of a few serviceable trunks'. But when in 1867 a Select Committee of the Otago Provincial Council (which also then controlled South Westland) recommended public reservation of surviving forest lands to prevent further 'wilful waste', the crucial debate was lost when West Coast representatives managed to argue that the timber was 'a great obstacle to the settlement of the country...and we should be permitted to destroy it without being interfered with by unnecessary legislation'.

The most influential voice for the creation of a park in New Zealand along the lines of Yosemite or Yellowstone was the painter and politician Sir William Fox, who was Premier of New Zealand on several occasions between 1856 and 1873. He toured the United States in 1852 and 1865, including a visit to Yosemite Valley. But it was the 1872 legislation creating Yellowstone Park which especially caught his attention, since he saw in this step a

The great touring geologist Ferdinand von Hochstetter made some perceptive comments on the geology of the Tongariro volcanoes in 1859. These comments were published in his widely read book, New Zealand and its Physical Geography, in which this chromolithograph appeared.

William Fox's naive technique in painting reflects a primitivism which in some ways was more honest than the picturesque style of the time. This painting was entitled Pohipis Pah, Tapueharuru Taupo, 1864. Ruapehu and Tongariro are seen in the background.

very real relevance to the North Island thermal districts. In 1874 he made a tour of the central North Island volcanic plateau and later wrote to the then Premier about the United States initiative in acting to protect such areas for wider public enjoyment. In March 1875 Fox set out for Europe intending to visit California on the way to do some paintings which were to include a series on Yosemite. Before he sailed from New Plymouth he lunched with Frederick Carrington, the Provincial Superintendent. The upshot was that two weeks later Carrington issued an order reserving from sale all forest and mountain land within a five mile radius of the crater of Taranaki/Mt Egmont.

With the first developments of tourism under way and more overseas visitors coming to New Zealand, there was growing concern that the natural attractions of the country should be protected from exploitation by individuals. In 1885 a 'Recreation Reserve' was created at Mount Cook which, in the words of the local Commissioner for Crown Lands (John H. Baker), was intended 'to conserve for all time a place whose beauties would not be easy to exaggerate, and will undoubtedly become one of the attractions of the globe'. The thermal areas of the central North Island, the Pink and White Terraces at Tarawera, and the volcanic mountains Tongariro, Ngauruhoe and Ruapehu were other obvious tourist drawcards. A book written by J. K. Nicholls in 1884, after his travels through 'the unknown region ruled over by the Maori King' revealed that this central North Island region was 'marvellous country...to all intents and purposes a terra incognita...a region designed, as it were, by the artistic hand of Nature'. And his conclusion was that with the 'Te Pakaru plain proclaimed as a public domain New Zealand would possess the finest park in the world'. Nicholls' Te Pakaru plain focused on the Tokaanu-Tongariro region. Nicholls' book was widely read in official and parliamentary circles in Wellington, as well as by the general public and was the first specific call for a public park since Fox's suggestion in 1874.

In 1884, however, the land still belonged to its Maori owners and Horonuku Te Heuheu had no interest whatsoever in selling. His acceptance of the idea of a gift to the nation two years later thus involved a considerable change of position. Besides his desire to keep the mountains sacred he almost certainly saw the gift as a means of restoring his own mana, as well as that of his tribe, in the eyes of the Government, after the Tuwharetoa's involvement in the Waikato land wars on the losing side and the sheltering of the fugitive rebel Te Kooti Rikirangi.

Although he was paramount chief, Te Heuheu could not transfer the lands in question without the cooperation of other Tuwharetoa chiefs. A special meeting of the Tuwharetoa was held at Rotoaira and the matter was widely debated. All finally consented that Te Heuheu would speak on their behalf and be the one to gift the land to the Crown; or as the Tuwharetoa would express it: 'Mau e tuku te taonga nei ki te karauna'. Accordingly, as a preliminary a brief document of intent was laid before the court, while arrangements were initiated to transfer some 6500 acres (2630 ha) from other local chiefs to Te Heuheu. At this stage the land in question comprised only three small circles drawn around the main volcanic craters – apparently by a random 'fling of a pair of compasses', but excluding the western slopes of Ruapehu which were always recognised as coming within the boundaries of the upper Wanganui tribes under Peehi Turoa and others. On 23 September 1887, a proper deed of gift was drawn up in the court at Taupo and the land became the property of the Crown.

Barely was the ink dry before a series of legal challenges began to the whole Taupo-nui-a-tia settlement, and therefore, by implication, to the validity of Te Heuheu's gift. The day following the signing of the deed a court order set aside a 20-acre block containing the Ketetahi Hot Springs. These had long been used by the Maori for treating a variety of ailments, and still remain separate from the park today, in spite of many attempts over the years to include them. More fundamental challenges came from Te Rangihiwinui Taitoko (Major Kemp) and the Wanganui tribes, who claimed that they had been disadvantaged by being involved in other Land Court proceedings at the same time. And a petition from Marton challenged Te Heuheu's basic claim to the mountains, let alone his right to cede them to the Queen 'as a land for sport'.

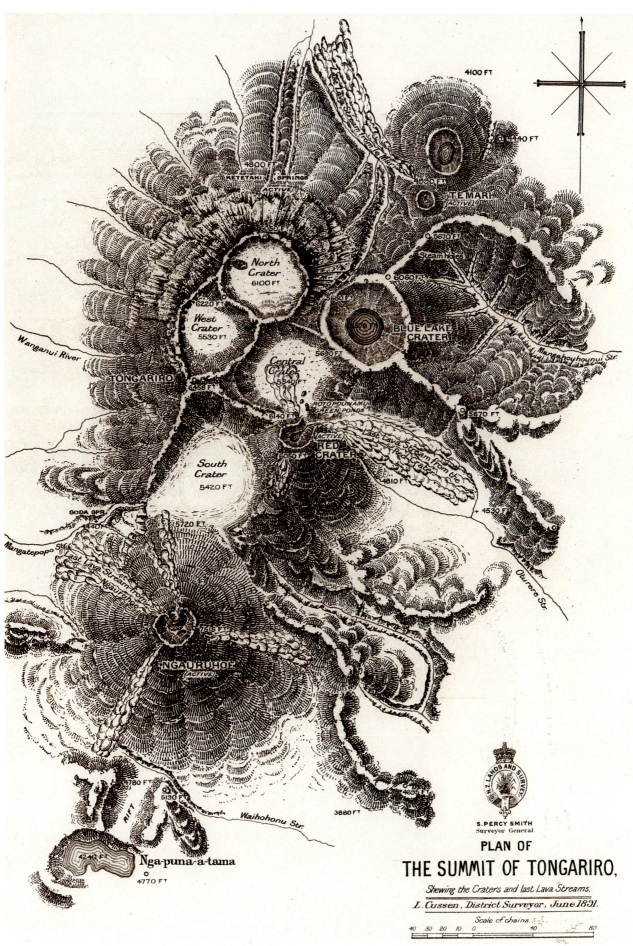

Lawrence Cussen completed the first detailed topographical survey of Tongariro in 1891. He was unable to establish a trig station on Mt Ngauruhoe because the mountain was in a constant state of tremor.

All these claims were dismissed by the Chief Judge of the Land Court in January 1888, opening the way for the Government to begin buying up land as additions to the proposed park. From the day of the deed it had been recognised that the size of the land involved was far too small and over the next few years, therefore, the Crown set about buying up adjoining lands. In this they were kept up to their task by Dr A.K. Newman, the Member of Parliament for Thorndon, who became the most prominent and persistent figure in ensuring that a park did in fact eventuate from Te Heuheu's gift. As a result the 'three detached blocks' were linked together and extended by additional purchases to form a 'dumb-bell' of land almost ten times the size of the original gift, but still very much confined to the highest country surrounding the summits of the main volcanoes.

In June 1893 the Tongariro National Park Bill was introduced by the Minister of Lands and became law in October 1894, providing for a park of some 62,350 acres (25,000 hectares), although the final conclusion of all land acquisition within the legislated boundaries was not completed until 1907. The park now existed clearly enough in both the eyes of the law and the minds of the nation, but its definition on the ground remained the rather unsatisfactory result of these diverse and tangled land dealings – a geometrically tidy boundary of circles and straight lines on the map which bore little or no relationship to the natural features of the region.

Worse still was the fact that while these original boundaries included landforms which had close counterparts elsewhere in the world, the plants and animals which gave the mountains their unique New Zealand quality belonged for the most part to the middle and lower slopes, and were thus excluded. Left beyond the borders of the park were most of the grasslands, the fine forests on the south side of Ruapehu and northern flanks of Tongariro, and the desert regions to the east. Much of the history of the succeeding decades involved a long saga of often frustrated efforts to rationalise and further extend these original park boundaries. And the recurrent boundary issues for their part frequently served to sharpen focus on two other major themes which always seem to simmer away at the core of significant questions concerning national parks. Why do we have them? And how do we manage them?

The first of these issues was thrown under the spotlight in 1907 when E. Phillips Turner and Dr Leonard Cockayne made a comprehensive topographical and botanical survey of the Tongariro region. Turner was Inspector of Scenic Reserves, and Cockayne an eminent botanist and pioneer conservationist who had laid the foundations for the South Island's first national park at Arthur's Pass. In a report which was to become a definitive statement on much more than just the botany of the district, Cockayne wrote that the park boundaries were 'inadequate and inconvenient' and the park as a whole presented

> ...the curious anomaly of being practically without a tree...It must not be forgotten that mountain, river, lake, glacier and even hot spring are much the same the world over, and that the special features of any landscape depend upon combinations of plants which form its garment, otherwise a monotonous uniformity would mark the whole earth...

After a thorough investigation Cockayne and Turner urged that the park be more than doubled in size by the addition of a further 31,000 hectares. In effect this would provide a band of forest, scrub, grassland and desert encircling the original 'dumb-bell' of bare scoria mountains. Their report was the start of a long campaign, which has gone on more or less continuously ever since, to extend the park boundaries to what many have considered to be their logical limits – the Desert Road in the east, the Main Trunk Railway in the south and west, and a combination of Highway 47 and Rotoaira Road in the north. Typical of the kind of sentiments behind these efforts were those reported in the Wellington *Evening Post* in October 1913:

> The very existence of the park is threatened by advancing saw-milling operations...The cutting out of the timber means driving a wedge into the girdle of growth without which

OHAKUNE FIRES

There were bonfires on the hillsides
in those days, high
above the raw-boned town
and trees and men giants against the sky
grappling for mastery—not men but bushmen took
their slashers in to hack
blazes on the beech trunks
smacking up a track of sorts,
forced a way to the ridge and stood
straight up to breast the trees
defeated, famished
in the thinning air.

Back on the farm on milder hills
they clubbed second growth
and lit their necessary fires;
women came—sometimes a child
screaming when the blazing
raced up close.
Dark, and
the booze began, tall tales
of men and bullocks gulped down
in twenty feet of mud or some
such thing in grandad's roaring time.
Round them the spit and snore
of logs' red bodies,
later the blundering
journey home (one, a neighbour,
drunken-drowned in the freezing stream).
And all the time
the hard stars riding by.

Time, it's a moving stage—
bonfires still blaze
and we hold out our hands
across a widening space
calling, hearing now only
the faint snap of the burning
and the far-off pack-a-pack
of the axes.

Lauris Edmond

Waihohonui Hut, built by the Tourist Department at the base of Mt Ngauruhoe in 1903, catered for a steady stream of early tourists.

Bullock team of the Taupo Totara Timber Company clearing the forest surrounding the park in 1912.

The railway gave the opportunity for all classes of people to gain ready access to the borders of the park. A 'K' class locomotive hauls a north-bound goods train across the famous Hapuawhenua Viaduct just north of Ohakune in 1949.

Army engineers helped build the Ohakune mountain road which snakes up to the Turoa skifield.

Members of Sir James Gunson's household view Mt Ngauruhoe erupting in 1928. Sir James was the mayor of Auckland from 1918-22, and forced along the campaign to open up the park to city people.

the park would be utterly desolate. The destruction is also certain to have a bad influence on waterways and to prejudicially affect land far richer in the lower valleys. An initial mistake was made in defining the boundaries of the park, for they were not sufficiently far-flung...

This is no place to catalogue the gradual growth of the park to its present 76,000 ha (three times its original size), nor the arguments and events which over the years have prompted or thwarted that growth. External circumstances like the advent of the Auckland-Wellington Main Trunk Railway (which from 1908 made the park far more readily accessible to the large populations in those two cities) and world wars clearly had a considerable influence at certain stages. But for the most part internal machinations of the bureaucratic process hobbled the pace of change, and positive action almost invariably lagged a considerable distance behind public feelings and pressures. People who cared about the Tongariro landscape were constantly calling for better boundaries, but those boundaries were woefully slow to eventuate. The temptation is to excuse some of the procrastinations on the grounds that a national park philosophy was not then sufficiently clearly formulated. Yet even today when that philosophy is both plainly stated and enshrined in statute, proposed additions to national parks which receive a large measure of public and scientific support are still often painfully slow to be given the stamp of official approval.

Since a centennial tends to be a time of celebration and self-congratulation, it is perhaps also salutary to remember times when things could have been done much better. With the benefit of hindsight the arguments for extending the original limited boundaries of the Tongariro National Park seem almost self evident. Firstly, there was Cockayne's basic conservation ethic, that what was unique to this part of the world was first and foremost its flora and fauna. Secondly, since only limited fringe areas 'were of any significant value for

An eruption of Mt Ngauruhoe in 1948.

milling and farming' these activities were not really in major competition with the goals of people like Cockayne. (This was to become a pattern for New Zealand national parks which by and large have been created in economically less important mountain regions while the biologically richer lowland and coastal areas have been surrendered to the axe and plough.) Thirdly, even in those areas which did have such value, the claims of the miller and farmer 'were in any case overridden by a number of vastly more important considerations' which included catchment protection and the fact that 'increasing tourist interest gave the local scenery a real and growing monetary value'. And finally there was a clear indication that 'the park cause was supported by many vigorous and influential individuals, by the newspapers, by a large segment of local opinion, and by much of officialdom'. Why then did the very necessary boundary extensions occur so woefully slowly?

The passages quoted in the preceding paragraph are taken from an unpublished Masters thesis by W.W. Harris (see BIBLIOGRAPHY) which examines the evolution of three of New Zealand's national parks, beginning with Tongariro. It is a lively and often entertaining account, and deserves a wider audience. In the concluding chapter Harris leaves no doubt at all that the main reason for the ineptitude in matters of boundary reform was

> ...the infuriating slowness of bureaucracy. First, during the Massey years, there had to be absolute certainty that the land being added to the park had no economic value. The resulting delay meant that by the time the movement into forests did begin in earnest the millers had become well entrenched, the State Forest Service had become more covetous of its own interests, and the Maoris had gained a healthier appreciation of property values. In consequence, attempted advances frequently generated into trench warfare, and matters were not assisted by the Lands Department's determination to acquire

Over 50 years ago a few hardy individuals walked and skied around the park. Two gentlemen display different turning styles on a trip from the Outuere Valley to Red Crater.

Salt Hut at the top of Bruce Road serviced skiers from the 1930s onwards.

Cyril Ellis surveys a wrecked carriage from the Tangiwai disaster. His story is told in the section on lahars in the volcanism chapter.

everything at the least possible cost, by the tendency to lose sight of difficult problems, by procrastination over such simple things as boundary surveying and timber inspection, and by conflict within the Department between park administration and responsibility for land settlement.

The net result was of course a long saga of 'Empire unachieved' – a catalogue of lost opportunities.

Fortunately some of these opportunities were not totally lost, and as recently as 1984, 3083 ha of Erua forest was added to the park and extensions to include parts of Rangataua forest are well in hand.

The creation of Tongariro National Park in 1894 was not accompanied by any significant changes in the way the region was used. No provision was made for wardens or rangers (the first resident ranger was finally appointed in 1931) and the first Board of Trustees set up to manage the park from 1894 to 1907 (including, it should be added, such prominent persons as the Minister of Lands, Surveyor General, Director of the Geological Survey and the Chief of the Tuwharetoa) did not apparently feel the need for any meetings. The first park board was appointed in 1907 and dissolved in 1914 when the park was passed to the tourist department. In 1922 a new board was created. Folk less burdened by serious public matters were, however, showing increasing interest in exploring the volcanic mountains, and to meet this demand the Government provided tracks and huts at Waihohonu in the east in 1901, and into the Ketetahi Hot Springs on the northern side of Tongariro in 1903.

It needs to be remembered that at this time the central volcanic massif was still a very isolated part of New Zealand. The Desert Road between Waiouru and Tokaanu was not completed until 1894, and it was 1908 before the Main Trunk Line was finally linked up just south of National Park. The advent of this railway was especially significant since its completion meant that the western side of the park was suddenly accessible to a much wider cross-section of the population. To meet the growing recreational demands this brought, a track and hut were built in the Mangatepopo Valley in 1918, intended mainly to cater for skiers and climbers on Mt Ngauruhoe. Two years later a dray road was pushed up through the forests in the Whakapapa Valley. A collection of tourist huts soon appeared at the head of this road, joined in 1929 by the Chateau Tongariro. Still higher up the mountain the Ruapehu Ski Club, in 1923, opened a hut on the ski slopes at 1770 m, although for the next 15 years skiers still had to walk to enjoy their sport until the first rope-tow on Ruapehu began operation in 1938.

In the last fifty years skiing has grown from these early pioneering efforts to a very large scale tourist industry, one which not only dominates much of Mt Ruapehu itself but also the way in which many people think of this whole national park, and indeed the way in which a significant number of the park staff employ their time. High level roads now lead to the ski fields at Whakapapa, Tukino and Turoa, terminating in mountain villages and a plethora of lifts spread over large parts of the mountain. In winter, skiers daily flock to these fields in their thousands bringing with them many of the demands of urban living into the national park and onto the sacred mountains.

How easily this kind of development can coexist with the national park ethic as it has evolved over the past 100 years is one of the main preoccupations of the final chapter in this book. Here we are only really concerned with unravelling a few of the main historical threads in the evolution of Tongariro National Park, and assessing, with the benefit of hindsight, how in the past we have managed to relate to the schemes of Nature in what was the first of our national parks. And it would appear that if this history teaches us anything it is surely that the judgements and opinions of the times are not necessarily infallible, even when the majority appears to be overwhelming.

In 1922, Parliament rewrote and revitalised the *Tongariro National Park Act*, at the same time making easily the most significant extensions to the boundaries of the park that have taken place at any one time since Te Heuheu made his original gift. History now applauds these acts, albeit both at the time were somewhat overdue. Yet in the same sessions the House saw fit to approve plans to convert the high volcanic plateau into a Scottish grouse moor for 'gentlemen shooters from the Old Country'. Horrific as this decision now seems to today's politicians and park managers (the poor grouse died without the help of shooters but the heather introduced with them became an appallingly noxious weed) only one solitary voice was raised in Parliament against what history has deemed 'gross desecrations of the indigenous landscape and horrendous violations of everything the National Park stood for'. Or, more simply, on the sacred mountains of Tongariro National Park

...until we introduced the heather and the foxglove and the lupin we had nothing but our own native plants, and very beautiful they are...

The historic site of Te Kooti's fortified pa at Te Porere, near the source of the Wanganui River, beneath Mt Tongariro. Te Kooti Rikirangi was a brilliant strategist and fighter during the land wars. Wrongly accused and imprisoned by the government, he escaped and fought many successful battles before making his last stand at Te Porere. Although defeated he evaded capture and established himself as the leader of the Ringatu church. He was finally granted official clemency.

The Tuwharetoa Marae at Waihi looks out over Lake Taupo.

'Here you may see that heart bared, see the process of the making and moulding of the land by fire, ice and water. Mother earth reveals her inmost secrets here; she pulses with never ceasing, sometimes fiery energy'.

James Cowan

'Increasingly we associate ourselves with our tools and our possessions, our science and our dreams. But we are inescapably still part of the natural world of plants and animals, of soils and air and water, a world which preceded us by billions of years and which will outlast our science and our species. National parks are the great cathedrals, galleries and museums of this natural world, as worthy of preservation as any edifice or achievement of our culture and civilization.'

Andy Dennis

'The Chateau was as monolithic as ever, still somehow appropriate. Not so the clutter around its flanks, like the unravelling of a piece of fabric. The village huddles uneasily around its giant spire in ecological discomfort.'

Geoff Rennison

The Chateau Tongariro has had a chequered career since building was commenced in 1929. It has been managed by private enterprise, the park, the Tourist Department and finally the Tourist Hotel Corporation and at one stage was even used as a mental hospital.

SACREDNESS AND PROTECTION

South Crater of Mt Tongariro.

SACREDNESS AND PROTECTION

Mt Ngauruhoe gathering night cloud.

'The time has come, not to forget, but to forgive ourselves the past, to begin again in humility to relate to our land.'

Peter Hooper *(Our Forests Ourselves)*

'You can't always get what you want, but if you try sometime you might just find, you get what you need...'

The Rolling Stones *(Let It Bleed)*

The centennial of Tongariro National Park provides us with a chance to reflect on the deeper implications of Te Heuheu's land-gift and the evolution of our present national park ideal. It is a timely opportunity to question what it means in today's world to regard mountains as 'sacred', and to examine the origins of the ideal of national parks and the way in which our generation treats this inheritance.

To set aside forever large areas of natural landscape and declare that nothing should be done to improve or exploit them is regarded as heresy by certain schools of thought, including some of the people who regularly make use of our national parks. Therefore, in order to protect these sanctuaries, a philosophy and vision is required that is both strong and forcefully enunciated. Furthermore to maintain the continued practice of such a philosophy will demand the energies and vigilance of individuals and groups. Many of these individuals and groups will speak from outside the national park bureaucracy. They will act as Socrates did, like gadflies on the establishment and at times win little praise for their purist attitude. But without them the national park vision will be eroded.

In this final chapter we shall explore the meaning of the land as 'sacred' and the ideals that national parks can stand for. It is only by constant reflection on these philosophical themes that the park will be protected for the next 100 years.

Mt Ruapehu at dusk. The lights are from ski huts at Whakapapa.

MYTHS OF POWER

The two most enduring myths of the central North Island volcanoes have been told in many forms. Here the story of the Tuwharetoa's ancestral tohunga Ngatoro-i-rangi bringing volcanic fire to New Zealand is related from Margaret Orbell's book *The Natural World of the Maori* and the story of the fighting warrior mountains is quoted from John Grace's book *Tuwharetoa*.

NGATORO-I-RANGI BRINGS VOLCANIC FIRE

Volcanic activity also had its origin in Hawaiki. It was brought here by the great tohunga, Ngatoro-i-rangi, who arrived on the Arawa canoe and set out with his slave, Ngauruhoe, to explore the countryside. When he reached Lake Taupo he climbed Mount Tauhara, by the north-eastern shore, and from its summit he cast his spear into the water; it turned into the trunk of a tall totara tree which stood there for many generations. He then descended to the shore of the lake. Finding there were no fish in it, he performed a ritual, then shook his cloak over the waters. From the strips of flax that fell from it there sprang the inanga and the banded kokopu, two species of galaxias which now inhabit the lake.

When Ngatoro-i-rangi arrived at Taupo it was dark and stormy, but suddenly the clouds parted and he saw Mount Tongariro — that is to say, the two neighbouring peaks which are known to the Pakeha as Mount Tongariro and Mount Ngauruhoe. At once Ngatoro-i-rangi determined to climb to the far, white summit of the mountain. As he and his slave made their way upwards they were attacked first by wind, then by rain and sleet and lastly by snow, but they would not give up, and in the end they stood upon the topmost peak. It was icy cold and they were in danger of freezing to death, so Ngatoro-i-rangi shouted to his two sisters to bring him fire.

The sisters, who were back in Hawaiki, heard his call and set out at once. They rested and lit a fire at Whakaari (White Island), which is now an active volcano in the Bay of Plenty, and then they made their way underground to Tongariro; sparks fell from their fire at Waiotapu, Ohaki, Rotokawa, Tapuaeharuru, and Tokaanu, creating the hot springs, geysers and boiling mud pools now to be found in these places. At Tongariro the sisters' fire warmed Ngatoro-i-rangi but came too late to save the life of his slave, Ngauruhoe; the crater of the mountain became his tomb, and its peak is known by his name. Then Ngatoro-i-rangi took the fire and hurled it into the crater, where it still burns. His sisters returned to the Bay of Plenty, again going underground and this time travelling further to the north and initiating as they went the thermal activity at Waimahana, Whakarewarewa, Ohinemutu and Tikitere. Some say that the fiery subterranean channels they formed are still in existence.

THE TALE OF THE WARRIOR MOUNTAINS' LOVE FOR PIHANGA

In the days when the world was young an assemblage of great mountains stood in the heart of the Ika a Maui (North Island). They were gods and warriors of great strength. They were so placed that Mount Egmont stood to the southwest of Ngauruhoe, Tongariro's most fierce volcano, where the lakes of Nga Puna a Tamatea now lie, and Tauhara and Mount Edgecumbe to the northeast where Lake Rotoaira now stretches like a sea.

In her robe of rich forest green, a little to the northwest of Tauhara, stood the fair mountain Pihanga. Her fame and beauty had spread to the far corners of the land; and each of the four mountains wooed her and wished her to be his wife.

Softly she would answer their words of love by an ascending column of mist that arose from about her, smiling and gold-bordered by setting sun. She adored them all and filled the fiery hearts of her four giants. Their joy filled the heavens with majestic outbursts and covered the earth with fiery lava and molten stones. She was undecided as to whom she would marry; and the snows of the winter and the suns of the summer came and went, and still she remained undecided.

Beautiful to behold from all the land was the great love of the giants; now all mantled with glistening snow, now hiding in clouds and bursting forth, covered with strange and wonderful beauty; now girdling their bodies with clouds and lifting their heads into golden heavens; and now and again breaking forth into terrible passions, covering the earth with blackness.

Pihanga aroused the passions of the giants; she made the volcanoes tremble! They became jealous of one another. Streams of lightning pierced the nights, and black smoke of deadly hate darkened the days as their voices roared insults at each other. They beheld the beauty of Pihanga as she smiled at them all.

The giants had decided to fight for the hand of the fair maiden, and there followed days of long silence. They stood grim and silent to the world, but they were gathering strength. They melted stones deep down in their bowels, and lit terrible fires—their powerful weapons. Then there came a day when a rumbling grew into the nights and filled the days; louder and louder, night after night, day after day—a groaning deep and dire. Suddenly a crashing thunder shook the earth, and from the mouth of Tongariro a fiery mass of molten stones burst forth. The battle had begun.

The battle raged for many days and many nights, but in the end Tongariro emerged victorious. He became the Supreme Lord over the land and the proud husband of Pihanga. In the days that followed he became the Sacred Mountain of Taupo; his handsome face captured the hearts of all; and he became the possessor of the highest tapu. The eyes of the new-born were directed towards him, and those of the departed rested full upon him as they went their way to the Gathering Place of Souls.

The defeated mountains debated among themselves as to where they should go. They said to one another, 'This is now the domain of Tongariro and we must depart. Let each of us go our way and find domains where we can rule undisturbed.' Mount Egmont said, 'I will follow the path of the setting sun and establish myself at its setting place!' Then Tauhara and Mount Edgecumbe said, 'As you shall follow the setting sun, so shall we travel to the sea where we can look toward the dawn.'

So they departed, and, bidding farewell to Pihanga, they started on their magic pilgrimage travelling under cover of darkness. In those days mountains were required to complete their full journey in one night. Mount Egmont (Taranaki) travelled westward, and in the morning found himself where that mountain now stands. Tauhara and Mount Edgecumbe journeyed eastward, but Tauhara moved very slowly as he was sad and sore at heart. As morning was close at hand his companion could not wait and decided to get to the sea as quickly as possible. Instead of continuing eastward Mount Edgecumbe journeyed northwards, and when the rays of the morning sun rose he found himself at the northern end of the Kaingaroa Plains.

Tauhara travelled with lingering steps and paused many times to look back at Pihanga, and when the morning came it found him not many miles from where he started. He now stands near the northeastern shore of Lake Taupo, and looks broodingly across at Pihanga and her proud husband.

Taranaki now looks eastward, quiet and brooding on revenge. One day, perhaps, he will rise up and come back in a direct route to fight Tongariro, and not follow the winding path—the Whanganui River—that he took when he left the realms of Tongariro. Tauhara and Mount Edgecumbe, that day, may also rise up and loosen their bonds with the earth and break the lands asunder. Who knows?

The andesitic volcano of Taranaki / Mt Egmont from the summit of Mt Ruapehu. Not all of Mt Ruapehu was included in Tuwharetoa land. The Maori people that look up to the south western slopes of Ruapehu have a saying:

Ruapehu te maunga,
Wanganui te awa,
Te Atihau nui a papa rangi
te iwi

Ruapehu is the mountain,
Wanganui is the river,
Te Atihau nui a papa rangi
are the people

The Crater Lake of Mt Ruapehu in winter.

SACREDNESS

Mt Ngauruhoe from the south.

Mountains, and especially volcanoes, are recalled in ancient tribal stories as great forces in a universe where everything is alive. They are seen as atua and are thus places of spiritual forces which command and give life to the natural world. Their wild and capricious actions can create and destroy on a huge scale. Accordingly, they are usually regarded with respect and humility, as well as with awe. To appease these greater-than-human forces a sacrifice or an offering was often required, or a tapu respected.

This is not peculiar to the Maori. It seems that most tribes and cultures living in the shadow of volcanoes have treated them as sacred, and many still do. A Japanese businessman still places food and a cigarette or two as an offering to the volcanic peak he is about to step upon. Similar rituals and signs of reverence are played out the world over.

An elderly Tuwharetoa woman will only visit Ruapehu when the clouds are down, hiding the sacred summits. And a young Tuwharetoa male journeying across the landscape in a modern machine still holds in awe his sacred Tongariro. The core of such belief is a thousand-year-old tradition invoked by a strong sense of place:

> When I see that mountain I know I am home, it is my centre; and even though I see people clambering all over it, it is still my spiritual centre...

In the mythology of the Tuwharetoa the mountains of Tongariro National Park are central in many ways. They are their matua (or parent of the land), the centre of their mana, and the peaks are identified with their tupuna (or divine ancestors). Tohunga and elders relate creation stories of volcanic fire and sagas of mountain conflicts in which battles were so titanic that even the earth-mother, Papa, was split and scarred. Originally the power of fire was held by the sky-father, Rangi. But in the cosmic beginnings of life, when Rangi was pushed apart from Papa, the ability to make fire was stolen by their rebellious children. Rangi carried fire-generating sticks suspended from his neck, but Te Whiro, god of the wind, audaciously stole the original spark of earthly fire from his father. And two of the lesser children of Rangi, Ngarehu-o-ahirangi and Motumotu-o-rangi, were fire-children whose remains now reside in the carbonised tree-trunks found in volcanic regions.

In a further cycle of myths volcanic fire is seen as the periodic appearance of the underworld, most commonly in association with Ruamoko and his wife Hine-nui-te-po (Papa's sister). Ruamoko is frequently credited with the power of controlling the seasons; by his fire he creates the heat of summer, and by withdrawing that fire, the cold of winter. In Tuwharetoa tradition the volcanic summits are ruled by three supernatural chiefs – Te Riro, Taka and Taunapiki. Anyone who ignored or defied the tapu risked either being killed by these chiefs or at least placed under a spell.

This talk of sacred mountains is not confined to some past relationship the Tuwharetoa held with the peaks of Tongariro and Ruapehu. It is very much alive today as a spokesman for the tribe relates:

'In the shadow of these cones, we face mystery and cataclysm where nature is met on its own terms'.

Bill Hackett

Lahar mounds at Pukeonake.

We look upon the mountains with deep respect and reverence and a tinge of many other complementary emotions, pride certainly being one of them. Proud that they are ours – "Te ha o Taku Manawa". The breath of my mountain is my heart. And proud that they are bequeathed to the nation who as nature lovers accord them their deep respect. Our reverence for the mountains goes deeper in that in time with the essence of our genealogies, all life form originated from the same parents Papa-tu-a-Nuku, the earth mother, and Rangi, the sky father, so that man and all other life forms are in harmony with one another in the bonds of kinship.

Conditioned then with these affinital ties we look upon those mountains as ancestors and this relationship evokes memories of our human ancestors who once roamed and settled within the mountain's shadows centuries ago so that by these memories the past and the present mingle ensuring their continuity. We sing or chant, today, ancestral compositions paying them homage.

The death of a high chief is likened to the tip of a mountain having broken off. The stern anchor of the Arawa canoe, Te Rangi Haruru or Toka Turua, is firmly fixed on Tongariro with the prow anchor, Toka Parore, firmly fixed at Maketu giving rise to the saying "Mai Maketau ki Tongariro" implying thereby its unshakable stability.

In the context of this broad mythology the mana of Tongariro to a traditional Maori is immense. From Ketetahi, Te Maari, Red Crater, Ngauruhoe and Ruapehu the power of the mountain thunders away, spitting steam and disgorging rock. In all seasons of the year storms spiral out from the core of the shattered landscape, sweeping across inhospitable regions of snow and ice, tussock and desert. For a Maori the Rangipo desert, and especially Onetapu its barren centre, is a place of awesome power, and crossing it fraught with dangers. Only a high-born Maori and those local tribes who have reached an understanding with these powers are exempt from shielding their eyes from the tapu mountains. And fires are not to be made from their natural charcoal.

To the Tuwharetoa, who felt that the earth was alive, nothing was more sacred than their volcanoes. This was not an attitude shared by most Europeans. John Bidwill, the first pakeha to ascend Ngauruhoe, simply did not believe in tapu restrictions on mountain tops, and wrote (in 1840) in both patronising and disdainful terms of the angry Tuwharetoa chief who confronted him on his return from the climb:

> He did not appear in a particularly good temper, and after about five minutes' talk he suddenly arose from his seat, and began to walk up and down, and stamp, talking all the time with great animation. He at last worked himself apparently into a most terrible pitch of fury, at which I only laughed. The cause of complaint was my having ascended Tongariro. I said that a Pakiha could do no harm in going up, as no place was taboo to a Pakiha; that the taboo only applied to Mowries; and finally that if the mountain was an atua, I must be a greater atua, or I could not have got to the top of it, and that it was all nonsense to put himself in a passion with me, as I did not care for it; but that if he would see that the people made haste with the canoe, I would give him some tobacco. I then took out one fig for each of his companions, who sat still all the time without saying a word, and gave him three figs. It proved a most astonishing sedative. He quite changed his tone in a minute and sat down again. He could not help saying, however, that if he had thought I could have gone up the mountain, he would have prevented me ever trying it, and requested me not to tell any other Pakihas of it on any account.

Even an explorer like Kerry Nicholls, who was much more sensitive to Maori beliefs and practices, could be deliberately disrespectful of the tapu on the mountains when it stood in the way of his own plans. Like Bidwill, he does not appear to have believed in its power, but was rather more careful about not offending his hosts:

> When entering upon the journey, I determined to follow a certain line of action throughout. I resolved to ascend Tongariro, to scale the summit of Ruapehu, and then to

Onetapu—the sacred centre of the Rangipo Desert.

enter the King Country at its furthest extremity, and return northward to Alexandra by the best route by which I could secure the most extended knowledge of the region to be traversed. If turned back by the natives at one point, I was prepared to try another. I was determined that no efforts should be spared to accomplish my object, and that no obstacle should impede my progress, save forcible opposition. To guard as much as possible against an occurrence of the latter kind, I resolved, above all when in contact with the tribes, to go fearlessly among them, to respect their customs, and follow, as near as possible, their mode of life, and, in fact, for the time being to become a Maori. Only in one instance was I forced to break through this rule, and that was in order to accomplish the ascent of Tongariro. This mountain, as before pointed out, is strictly tapu, and I was aware that all the persuasive diplomacy in the world would not secure me permission to ascend it; I therefore had to accomplish this task unbeknown to the Maoris having settlements in its vicinity.

After Bidwill many Europeans came to climb the sacred mountains. At first the local Maori, who would not see their mountains desecrated, turned all away (including, in 1850, the then Governor, Sir George Grey), even though some did manage to sneak up unobserved. Before too long, however, Maori culture was struggling with a different kind of fire as the Land Wars erupted across the face of the North Island. Weight of numbers and guns on the European side prevailed and for a time the beliefs and the people felt conquered, crushed and dispirited. The main loss was their land. In the aftermath of these defeats it was inspired thinking that led a warrior chief to safeguard the sacred peaks by presenting them as a gift to the Crown. At least as a national park something of the tapu might be preserved, if only symbolically.

For Horonuku Te Heuheu the central question of how to preserve the sacredness of land which gave so much essential meaning to the tribe as a source of identity and mana was part of an even wider culture shock. Not only was the power balance changing on earth but also in the heavens – the fact that they had been subdued by another culture was inevitably linked by the Maori to the power of the Europeans' god. Ironically this god not only held dominion over all nature and allowed no other gods or goddesses to be worshipped, but was also portrayed as a suffering, dark-skinned deity. This struck a deep chord in the Maori soul. Many in the tribe including Horonuku and other chiefs adopted with fervour a belief in the risen Jesus. Christian crosses were erected at the marae (some Maori say the crosses replace the old tapu pole with a new more powerful tapu) and masses, eucharists and sermons spread the new spirit. Although missionary zeal and the alienation felt by the conquered race suppressed some traditional spirituality, many older practices and divine beings were enveloped into the new faith, or simply not forgotten in a defiant pagan stance.

Today Maoridom has survived a crisis of faith in traditional values and is undergoing a renaissance, but there are still powerful forces unsettling the Maori sense of place and tapu. Young people leave the tribe for the cities where secular education and mass media do little to promote spiritual values. This time the seduction away from traditional beliefs is not by an apparently more profound and powerful spirituality, but by a combination of disillusionment and rapid change which goes with progress. Traditional concepts like mana and tapu die fairly swiftly in a society which worships instead consumer goods, fast city life, excitement and freedom. The tribe and its beliefs are overrun in the souls of many individuals as surely as the suburbs of Auckland have overlaid the volcanoes of Hauraki.

Of course this estrangement from tradition and place, spirit and authority is not a uniquely Maori dilemma. The pakeha's faith in absolutes is undergoing a similar collapse. Contemporary society shares no single spiritual world-view. Such is the extent of this modern secularism that little seems to be sacred anymore. As far as the spirit of the mountains is concerned there are no shared sacred responses outside the Maori marae. While some of us may bow in spirit to wild places, we have no acceptable forms to bow in body, no ritual ceremonies to join in, no ways to pay homage.

Kaikawaka, during a break in a snowstorm.

Perhaps for most people such a secular atmosphere is entirely appropriate. They no longer believe in a god or spiritual power existing behind geological, meteorological and psychological processes. Moreover, religious dogmas are seen as being directly implicated in the destruction of the biosphere, the subjection of women and racial groups, and a host of other major contemporary problems.

Yet it is one of the more admirable qualities of modern democracy that it seeks to protect the full range of beliefs held by its citizens. The popular American wilderness philosopher Edward Abbey argued at the beginning of *Desert Solitaire* that 'the personification of the natural is exactly the tendency I wish to suppress in myself, to eliminate for good'. Yet there are few greater defenders than Abbey of those parts of the wilderness which others hold to be sacred (such as Indian power spots, or the mountain atua of the Maori). If a significant minority believe that some places are sacred and deserving of special recognition then the rights of those who so believe should be respected and those places protected. This is especially so in the case of a bicultural society where the concept of sacredness may have a diversity of meanings.

Today a new pride in their ancestral beliefs is returning to the Maori; so is a new voice to express old ways. In this resurgence they are looking again to their sacred mountains. The present paramount chief of the Tuwharetoa, Sir Hepi Te Heuheu describes it as follows:

> Our people want to go back to the feet of the mountain. It is a part of our relearning our Maori way. But we are not sure how to approach Tongariro; it is difficult to know which way is right anymore. When we organised a trip with Bruce Jefferies, the chief ranger at the national park, some of our elders were not keen on coming because of the tapu. Others did not want to go far up the mountain. You must understand that although most of us are Christians we have not forgotten our Maori ways. The old ladies on the bus, they recited Maori prayers all the way while we approached the mountain. For some it was the first time they had been in the park, although they have lived near Taumaranui or Turangi most of their lives. Now we talk about it on the marae, and we will return on the day of the centennial and say a karakia to the mountains – our gift.
>
> But it is different when we go like this as a group, as members of the tribe, than as individuals. This is when we feel the mana and tapu strongest. This matter of tapu is important. We want to see people enjoy the mountain but we do not want it desecrated. Some of our people feel more strongly than others on this. Some would have no commercialism on the mountains at all, to others it is no great matter because it is Pakeha anyway. And yes, the tapu is still there, but it is no longer the kind that kills. Now the gift is a Maori-Pakeha thing, and we want it to stay that way.

An unidentified worm at Silica Springs.

'The universe would be incomplete without Man; but it would also be incomplete without the smallest transmicroscopic creature that dwells beyond our conceitful eyes and knowledge'.

John Muir

Two and a half thousand years ago, when the Minoan, Egyptian and Chinese civilisations were well established, Ngauruhoe was born. A natural pyramid, it is a very young mountain, hence its innocence of form.

PROTECTION

For at least the last 3000 years western societies have largely regarded wild nature as repugnant and evil. In many religions and philosophies, but most especially in the Judeo-Christian tradition, nature has been seen to represent the uncontrolled, bestial elements of human behaviour which need to be repressed by a disciplined moral code. That which is civilised, cultivated and controlled is good (and therefore God's will), whereas that which is primitive, uncultivated and uncontrolled is bad, and therefore the work of the Devil or ascribed to evil impulses. There were some remarkable exceptions to this sweeping generalisation (for example, Celtic culture and individuals like St Francis of Assisi). But in the main, nature only became pleasant and acceptable when people had dominion over it in domesticated pastoral settings or viewed from the comfort of the living room. The only parks or reserves created in these times were designed to keep the game in and the peasants out at the whim of the ruling class.

It was not until the advent of Romanticism in the eighteenth century that the great antipathy to wilderness was partially overcome. This revolution in the Western attitude to wild nature was caused by the coalescence of a number of social movements. Scientific innovations revealed nature and the universe to be a vast, harmonious and ordered system. Industrialism and city life brought progress of a kind but also created squalor and pollution on a large scale. And the genius of a few poets discovered direct insights into sublime forces in wild places.

The awe and inspiration writers like William Wordsworth, Samuel Taylor Coleridge, Lord Byron and other Romantic poets felt on their long walks through the English Lake District and European Alps led them to a philosophy in which untouched nature became a wonderful imaginative stimulant to individual spiritual development. A similar enlightenment was occurring on the Continent where writers like the eccentric philosopher, Jean Jacques Rousseau, were arguing that modern man should import into his distorted urban existence primitive qualities learned from actually living close to nature.

In the nineteenth century places like the Alps or the Lake District were becoming increasingly scarce in the Old World but existed in almost limitless supply in the colonies. Probably the most sophisticated and articulate philosopher to take up the defence of wild nature in the New World was the American, Henry David Thoreau. Unlike the vast majority of his colonial countrymen who set out to subdue the new lands, Thoreau recognised a positive value in unspoilt wilderness. He reflected on the immense pleasure people can derive from observing even simple happenings in nature, like the slow opening of a flower. But more importantly, he argued that contemplation of nature leads to a transcending of physical appearances to spiritual truths. He wished to protect wilderness 'for modesty and reverence's sake, or if only to suggest that earth has higher uses than we put her to'. At the core of his thinking was the belief that as in nature our greatest human values are 'wild and free', summarised in his now famous saying: 'In wildness is the preservation of the world'.

By the time Thoreau was writing, wilderness had not only been devastated in England and most of Europe but was also fast diminishing in colonial lands. Accordingly, when the call to protect what was left began to filter out from the cities of Europe and the east coast of America, it was in the American West and other lands colonised by the English that the first preservationists began to achieve results. These new colonies were usually rich countries with youthful but strong democratic ideals and enough wild frontier to parcel out portions for some vague intangible 'benefit' for all their citizens.

The fact that the new positive feeling for wilderness became transposed into a reality ultimately owed more to the dedicated politicking of preservationists like John Muir than the philosophical reflections of people like Thoreau. Muir was neither a great writer nor a particularly astute philosopher – he simply loved wild places and fought long and hard to protect them. He wrote, lectured and lobbied and it was these efforts (and those of a few

During summer the National Park runs interpretation trips like this journey to one of the summits on Mt Ruapehu.

kindred souls like Frederick Olmsted) which led to the creation of Yosemite State Park in 1864, the first large reservation of a publicly owned wilderness for the complete protection of all flora and fauna and the enjoyment of everyone. On the heels of this initial success Muir formed the Sierra Club, the first citizen body to advocate wilderness protection and the model for many subsequent voluntary groups which still today take much of the initiative in creating new parks and imposing management constraints as public bureaucracies surrender to commercial pressures.

Thus a few sensitive thinkers wrote the poetry and thought the thoughts necessary to turn a fear of the wilds and utilitarian attitude to land on its head. A handful more followed thought with action. Yosemite however was only a state park, and the first public reservation belonging to a nation as a whole took place eight years after Yosemite at Yellowstone.

In 1870, Henry D. Washburn, Surveyor General of Montana, set out with a high-powered team of business and military men along with their packers and cooks. Despite an arduous journey Washburn reports that on seeing the valley of geysers 'our usually staid and sober companions threw up their hands and shouted with ecstasy at the sight'. It is also recounted that Cornelius Hedges, a lawyer among them, persuaded the group that

> ...there ought to be no private ownership of any portion of the region, but the whole ought to be set apart as a great National Park, and that each one of us ought to make an effort to have this accomplished.

Another in the group, Nathaniel Langsford, a banker and railway advocate, gave a series of lectures on the region. One of Langsford's lectures was attended by Ferdinand V. Hayden, head of the Geological Survey, who successfully petitioned Congress to put up $40,000 to survey the region.

The survey took place in 1871 with photographer William Jackson and Thomas Moran, a great painter of the Western Frontier, also in the party. Their photographs and paintings were later exhibited before Congress along with the glowing reports from both expeditions. The upshot was that in 1872, Congress, which had never visited the region nor even formally secured it from the Indians, gave Yellowstone to the nation as the world's first national park.

Words from the 1872 *Yellowstone Act* are still echoed today in national park legislation all over the world:

> The Yellowstone region is hereby reserved and withdrawn from settlement, occupancy, or sale...and set apart as a public park or pleasuring ground for the benefit and enjoyment of the people...The Secretary of the Interior shall provide for the preservation...of all the timber, mineral deposits, natural curiosities or wonders within the said park...in their natural condition...

By the time of Te Heuheu's gift of Tongariro National Park in 1887, Australia (in 1879) and Canada (in 1885) had also set aside areas for national parks. All looked to the Yellowstone arguments and legislation for their inspiration and other themes were also emerging. Although politicians were generally receptive of the ideals of national parks, no country moved with undue haste towards anything like responsible management of the areas it had so glowingly protected. For many people parks found most favour as objects of national pride in new countries which could boast no great cathedrals or works of human art, but could at least gain cultural points for the world's highest waterfall, tallest geyser, greatest glacier in a temperate region or grandest canyon. In other respects, however, it took decades of mismanagement (or no management at all) and terrible cases of destruction of flora, fauna and scenery before any government saw fit to establish effective legislation and provide an active ranger service. Thus from the time of their creation each park was assaulted by a battery of diverse and sometimes conflicting uses and abuses. In short, the early history of mismanagement of Tongariro as told in the previous chapter was paralleled

Industrial structures break the soft flow of natural lines.

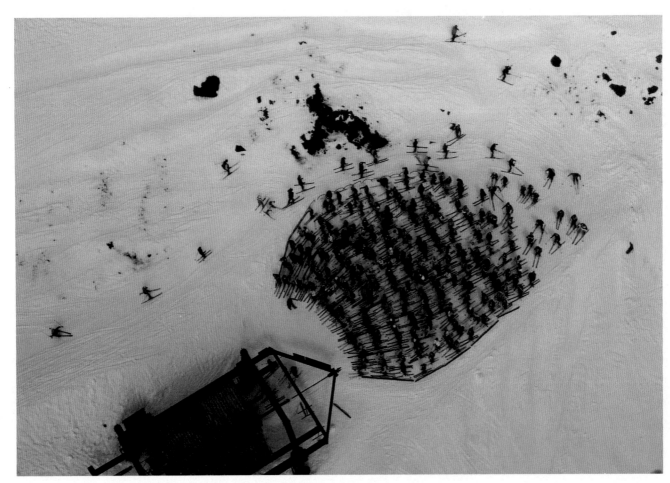
Rush hour at the tow queue.

in most other countries which followed the Yellowstone example. And the problems continue.

At Tongariro commercial concerns are plugging away relentlessly at park administrators to open up the park to larger ski areas, more lifts and gondolas, heliskiing, more luxurious accommodation, and generally more development in the name of customer numbers, comfort and thrills. It is not just the numbers of tourists (which will soon reach one million a year at Tongariro) but the impact of some of the services that is giving real cause for concern. Existing skifields have a high impact not only on the natural environment but also on park philosophy and activity. These days some rangers spend much of the winter tied to overseeing the skifields and carparks, and no longer have time for wider ranging duties. And the irony is that although it is sucked into this kind of high-impact commercial operation, the park itself reaps little financial reward. At Whakapapa skifield alone it costs the park, and therefore the taxpayer, a considerable annual subsidy to service skiing activities, money which is simply not recovered from concession fees and other levies and charges.

There is nothing new in calls for this kind of improvement, but neither is a healthy fear of them a recent phenomenon. In 1886, a United States Congressional Report on Yellowstone stipulated that 'the park should so far as possible be spared the vandalism of improvement'. What makes today's situation so disturbing is that although Congress clearly perceived the threat of overdevelopment (which it seems many park administrators in New Zealand fail to comprehend) it nevertheless still failed to stop it. And what are the consequences? Yellowstone is now besieged by roads crammed with motorcars, on-site accommodation, a plethora of facilities and a volume of people that everyone would agree is simply loving the United States largest park to death. The same kind of thing is happening in Grand Canyon National Park which reverberates to the sound of about 300 helicopter and small plane flights every day, totally destroying hikers' peace and serenity.

During the 1972 Yellowstone centennial celebrations the United States Park Service called together a citizens' commission to formulate a broad set of management priorities for the next one hundred years. This centennial task force gave highest priority to removing commercial concessions and private vehicles from within park boundaries. The United States Director of National Parks is at present supporting moves in the Federal Government to exclude aeroplane and helicopter flights from Grand Canyon. In other words, it has taken some Americans one hundred years to learn what Congress instinctively knew from the start – namely, that 'improvements' or 'enhancements' degrade the national park ideal.

Yet dominant voices in New Zealand park management seem to be following blithely down the same circuitous path as their American counterparts. For example, at a meeting of local residents at Taumaranui in the summer of 1985, Mr Roger Holyoake, the chairman of Tongariro National Park Board, listed possible developments which were blocked because of restrictions in the current management plan. These included heliskiing, a gondola on Whakapapa and even night skiing, schemes which he claimed would involve 'an enormous spin-off for our area'. At the same time the Hauraki Gulf Maritime Park was threatening to take legal action against helicopters landing on park islands. In the words of Chief Ranger Rex Mossman:

> there had been many complaints about the disturbance helicopters caused. Most people came to the park to enjoy the serenity of its islands and reserves. A helicopter carrying four passengers can affect a lot of people. I see it as a benefit for a few against a cost for many.

Certainly the serenity of the many was shattered long ago at Mt Cook National Park where ski planes continuously buzz the Tasman Glacier, the whine of their engines reverberating against the mountain walls. It is even worse in Westland National Park where the superb walk up the Fox Glacier past the huge ice pinnacles and ice caves and across the magnificent herbfields around Chancellor Hut is shattered on most fine days by a virtually continuous noise that would drive a modern worker to ear-muff protection.

What emerges from these contemporary examples is that New Zealand still lacks a clear philosophy of values for its national park management. If Tongariro emulates Hauraki and holds out against further major development within its boundaries, it may still appear to be shutting the barn door after the horse has bolted. But the situation is not irredeemable. Concessions can be removed to outside park boundaries. Further roading within national parks can be seen as inappropriate. The flying-over and landing of aeroplanes and helicopters can be restricted to specific limited areas, or denied altogether. However, to convince tourists, the public and themselves that these kinds of development are ultimately destructive of deeper and more fundamental values, park administrators will need to develop more coherently than they have at present a philosophy which recognises the full range of human and non-human values which they are trying to protect in national parks.

Cars, chairlifts, helicopters, gondolas – in fact any mechanised conveyances – distort or destroy a natural sense of the flow of time and space as irrevocably as they destroy the quiet that preceded them. Even too many tracks, signs and amenities can distance people from a natural encounter. Most people simply do not choose to go for a walk alongside a road, carry their skis uphill beside a chairlift, or contemplate the otherness of nature beneath the beating blades of a helicopter.

National parks are often the only sizeable places left on the planet where we still have the chance to legislate specifically against all such mechanised disturbances. That many people would readily agree to destroying this choice, even in national parks, only confirms the rather melancholy reflection that human nature often chooses the easiest and most comfortable way. Such people should, however, bear in mind that the comfort or thrills of the mechanised option are available without too much opposition over almost 90% of the New Zealand land area.

If in our bid for the local and international tourist dollar we turn our national parks into fun-parlours then those parks will become just one more packaged consumer experience, albeit partaken against a pretty backdrop. Worse, in so doing we will not only commit that 'vandalism of improvement' which the American Congress anticipated a century ago, but will also slowly relinquish our last chance to escape into solitude to experience a real, raw, and at times uncomfortable alternative to our everyday lives.

There is an ambivalence in the souls of each of us which perhaps goes right to the core of why modern societies need to legislate to protect wilderness. This ambivalence derives from the fact that we need both civilisation with all its comforts, and wilderness with all its discomforts. We are both social and solitary beings whose personalities, as much as our culture, derive from the interplay of the wild and the ordered.

Most often we need personal and social contact. We cling to our civilised values and gain knowledge and security from our conditioning even when we are cynical of some aspects of it. Yet if there is too much planning and order something inside us gets suffocated. There are occasions when we need a huge place where time and space is measured out by natural rhythms, and where we see, hear, taste and smell only what we can never create. In other words, times when we need the wilderness and its solitude.

Parks which hold to the wilderness philosophy continue to provide a place in which to live out the great whirl of evolution as a fighting animal. Between the forest and the tussock, under the huge mountains, we become lost to our civilised selves and free to re-create. Perhaps we re-create out of the long past and into the long future, ancestral and tribal, always strangers on an unfamiliar yet in many ways everyday earth. Perhaps we re-create out of a simple search inside our own heads. Either way, the anxiety may be immense – this is not always a time and place of comfort. There are no escapes by way of distractions to remove either your need for personal control or the huge forces of nature around you. No one pretends that wilderness is easy; but that was surely the very point of going there in the first place.

And so there is a sense in which parks are a giant meditation arena. The discipline is the walking (with a weight on your back), the sitting and waiting for weather to clear, and the

Free skiing on Tongariro.

Taranaki, we are still bound to you with ropes of love from Ruapehu, Ngauruhoe and Tongariro.

Tongariro.

Desert Road II.

For some artists in the nineteenth century, looking at nature become an act of devotion. The wild landscape most clearly represented, or in fact was, God's work. This transcendental philosophy was reflected in the 'picturesque' style of painting in which the wilderness was idealised and moralised just at the time that industrial frontier societies were destroying vast tracts of nature and driving most people toward the cities. Today artists, like all society, look out from their urbanised secular environments and see in national parks a world apart from human manipulation. They try to open doors of perception and discover serious ways of relating to untrammelled mother earth. A Tuwharetoa sculptor and painter, Albert McCarthy, incorporates material from the volcanic plateau in his works while the photographer, Gillian Chaplin, evokes anxiety and security, both human and wild in her image from the desert road.

keeping of a level head in fearful situations. The lesson is somewhere out there in the beauty and power of nature, and your coming by the hard road to a strong relationship with it. The insight and enlightenment, should it come at all, can be sudden or gradual, short or long, full of raving to companions or alone in the silence. But anyone who encounters the wilderness will return to their daily lives at least a little changed.

A society which destroys its wilderness is one which has destroyed one of the best aspects of its culture. National parks can be compared to museums, art galleries, temples, or even our bedrooms. They are, in the words of Edward Abbey, 'sanctums of our culture' where we shut off machines and enter in peace to encounter another side of reality. A gradual improvement of facilities, a compromise with a skifield here or a helicopter company there, and we may wake up tomorrow to find we have lost that other side.

In the Romantic period artists and poets reopened our eyes to wild places. Today they continue to give us images and words which go right to the heart of an understanding of wilderness. Not always easy words, but then wilderness is not always easy. All the same, perhaps a few of their enigmatic insights should begin more of our management plans:

> We shall not cease from exploration
> And the end of all our exploring
> Will be to arrive where we started
> And know the place for the first time.
> Through the unknown, remembered gate
> When the last of earth left to discover
> Is that which was the beginning...

T.S.Eliot (Little Gidding)

Islands of alpine tussock and shrubs caught in a vicious winter blizzard.

Lava blocks in the Oturere Valley.

In the forge of Red Crater.

'Te Ha O Taku Maunga Ko Taku Manawa—The breath of my mountain is my heart.'
Windshear cloud formation over Mt Ruapehu.

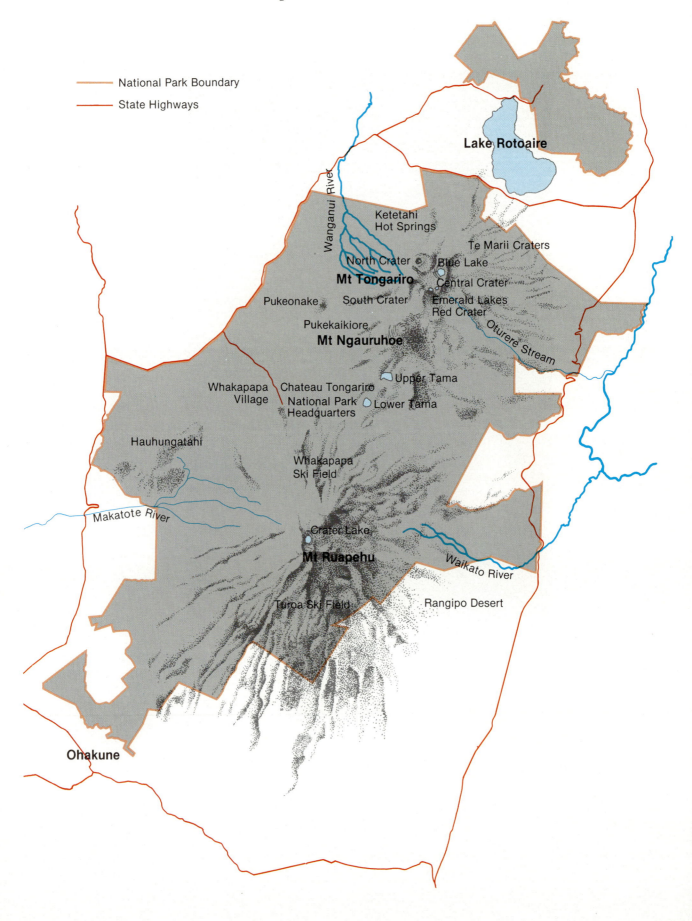

ACKNOWLEDGMENTS

Grateful acknowledgment is made to the Tongariro Park staff with special thanks to Bruce Jefferies and Paul Dale. Many people have helped with valuable information and comments on the text: Jim Cole, volcanology; Sue Weston and Margaret Orbell, history; Stephen Asher and Sir Hepi te Heuheu, Maori perspective; John Wheeler, Jon Jackson and Andy Dennis, general suggestions and comments.

PHOTOGRAPHS

Unless otherwise stated all the photos were taken by Craig Potton either with a Nikon FE2 using Kodachrome 64, 35mm film or an Asahi Pentax 6x7 camera using Ektachrome 64, 120 film. Other photographers' gratefully received contributions appear as listed:

Bruce Jefferies pp. 120, 172, 176
Gillian Chaplin p. 181
Albert McCarthy p. 180/1, 180/2
Lew Cormack p. 175
Herb Spannagel p. 18
Tongariro National Park Collection pp. 20, 21, 23
Lloyd Homer, Geological Survey p. 30
Beverly Baseman took the photo of the photographer on the jacket flap.

Black and White Images:
Tongariro National Park Collection pp. 140/1, 133
Veronica Black p. 137/2
Alexander Turnbull Library p. 140/2
Hall Raine collection p. 136/1, 136/2
New Zealand Railways; Courtesy, R. Jordan and N.Z. Railway and Locomotive Society Inc. p. 137
Wilson and Horton Ltd p. 141
Hocken Library, Dunedin, Burton Bros. p. 122
Auckland Institute and Museum pp. 128, 129

PAINTINGS

The following paintings are reproduced with the kind permission of the Alexander Turnbull Library:
George French Angas: 'Te Heuheu and Iwakau' p. 122, 'Volcano of Tongariro with Motupoi Pah' p. 124; 'The volcanic region of pumice hills looking towards Tongariro'; and 'Ruapehu' p. 125. (All three images were reproduced as lithographs by J.W. Giles.)
William Fox: 'Tapueharuru Taupo, Pohipi's Pah' watercolour p. 131/2
Ferdinand Von Hochstetter: 'Lake Taupo' p. 131/1

QUOTATIONS

Quotations used in the text, in order of appearance, are from the following sources:
Janet Frame, 1983—from *To the Is-land,* pub. The Women's Press in association with Hutchinson Group Ltd.
John Newton, 1985—*Opening the Book,* reproduced in the *New Zealand Listener.*
Kohine Whakarua Ponika—*He Waiata Murimuri-aroha,* pub. *The Penguin Book of New Zealand Verse,* 1985, Penguin.
Marshall Gebbie, 1971—*Tongariro,* The Journal of the Tongariro National Park.
George Walker, 1978—in an article 'Prospects of Catastrophe', *New Zealand Listener* 7 October 1978.
Hou Han Shui, *Herodian*—in *Tongariro,* The Journal of the Tongariro National Park.
Apirana Taylor, 1984—*The Womb,* pub. *The Penguin Book of New Zealand Verse,* 1985, Penguin.
Bruce Houghton—in *Tongariro,* The Journal of the Tongariro National Park.
James Kerry-Nicholls, 1884—in *The King Country.*
John Chase and Donald Gregg—in *Volcanoes of Tongariro National Park,* 1960 Donald Gregg.
Cyril Ellis—in *New Zealand's Darkest Days,* pub. *The New Zealand Herald.*
Lynn Davidson—'The Turning', pub. *New Zealand Listener,* 17 August 1985.
Sam Hunt—*A White Gentian,* published with permission of the poet.
John Grace—*Tuwharetoa, A History of the Maori People of the Taupo District,* pub. A.H. and A.W. Reed, Wellington, 1959.
John Bidwill, 1839—in *Rambles in New Zealand.*
James Cowan, 1929—*The Tongariro National Park.*
Andy Dennis, 1984—*The Alpine World of Mount Cook National Park.* Andy Dennis and Craig Potton, pub. Cobb Horwood.

Geoff Rennison—in *Tongariro,* The Journal of the Tongariro National Park.
Bill Hackett—in *Tongariro,* The Journal of the Tongariro National Park.
Dr. Leonard Cockayne, 1980—in *A Report on a Botanical Survey of Tongariro National Park,* Pub. N.Z. Parliamentary House of Representatives.
William Harris—in *Three Parks;* an analysis of the origins and evolution of the New Zealand National Park movement, M.A. Thesis, pub. University of Canterbury.
Peter Hooper, 1981—*Our Forests Ourselves,* pub. John McIndoe.
Margaret Orbell—*The Natural World of the Maori,* M. Orbell and Geoff Moon, pub. Collins, 1985.
Edward Abbey, 1968—*Desert Solitaire,* pub. Ballantine.
T.S. Eliot—*Collected Poems* pub. Faber and Faber Ltd.

We gratefully acknowledge permission of the Tuwharetoa to reproduce Waiata and other sayings.

FURTHER READING

John H. Grace, *Tuwharetoa; a history of the Maori people of the Taupo district.* A.H. and A.W. Reed, Wellington, 1959. An involved historical account. Out of print.

W.W. Harris, *Three Parks; An analysis of the origins and evolution of the New Zealand National Park Movement.* M.A. thesis, Geography Dept, Canterbury University. A superb political study of the evolution of Tongariro, Arthurs Pass and Westland National Parks.

Dr. Leonard Cockayne, *A Report on a Botanical Survey of Tongariro National Park,* N.Z. Parliamentary House of Representatives. A detailed description of park vegetation and the reasons for park extensions.

Karen Williams, *Volcanoes of the South Wind,* pub. Tongariro Natural History Society. A field guide to the forces of volcanism in Tongariro National Park.

Isobel Gabites, *Roots of Fire,* pub. Tongariro Natural History Society. A field guide to the ecology of Tongariro National Park.

The Tongariro National Park Handbook. The first handbook written in 1927 by James Cowan places great emphasis on Maori values, but is unfortunately out of print. The most recent handbook, *The Restless Land* by various contributing authors, was published in 1981.

GLOSSARY

The following Maori place names are loosely translated only but they do give some indication of the techniques of Maori nomenclature. Most are taken from James Cowan's original park handbook.

Hauhungatahi: occasionaly covered in snow.
Ketetahi: One basket (of food). The Maori sometimes cooked food by placing it in the boiling springs at Ketetahi.
Makatote: Stream of plentiful ferns.
Ngauruhoe: See myths of power, pages 156-157.
Onetapu and Rangipo: Place of darkness (dark sky of eruptions) and sacred sands.
Pihanga: A window-like opening in the roof of large houses to let out the smoke. The crater of Mt Pihanga is thought to resemble such an opening.
Pukekaikiore: Hill where rats were eaten—where the Tuwharetoa tribe defeated another and were purported to have eaten some of the vanquished, i.e. human rats.
Rotopounamu: Lake of deep green waters.
Ruapehu: Explosive sounding crater.
Tongariro: See myths of power, pages 156-157.
Whakapapa: To lay out flat like boards or flat rock. After an inter-tribal battle, the bodies of the defeated were laid out here before the feast.

The following Maori words are used in this book:
Atua: Spirit; supernatural
Mana: Influence; power
Ngati: People of ... (used with tribal names)
Tapu: Sacred; forbidden
Tohunga: Expert; specialist; priest
Tupuna: Ancestor

Potton, *Tongariro: A Sacred Gift*
ISBN 0-86866-110-4

Errata
p. 114, caption, *for* Kawakawa *read* Rangiora
p. 152, *photo is upside down*